RIVER LIFFEY

A CITY RUNS THROUGH THEM

A CITY RUNS THROUGH THEM

Dublin and its Twenty
River Bridges

FERGAL TOBIN

Atlantic Books
London

First published in hardback in Great Britain in 2023 by Atlantic Books, an imprint of Atlantic Books Ltd.

10 9 8 7 6 5 4 3 2 1

A CIP catalogue record for this book is available from the British Library.

Hardback ISBN: 978-1-83895-935-7
E-book ISBN: 978-1-83895-936-4

Printed in Great Britain

Design benstudios.co.uk

Map artwork by Jeff Edwards
Endpaper image: British Railways poster (London Midland Region), Dublin by Kerry Lee, 1954 (© *Science Museum Group*)

Atlantic Books
An imprint of Atlantic Books Ltd
Ormond House
26–27 Boswell Street
London WC1N 3JZ

MIX
Paper | Supporting responsible forestry
FSC
www.fsc.org
FSC® C171272

i.m. Nora Pigott (1914–2006)
my mother

*The business of Dublin is to show its
face to England and its arse to Kildare.*

Richard Killeen, attrib.

CONTENTS

PREFACE AND ACKNOWLEDGEMENTS

UNLIKE MY PREVIOUS book, *The Irish Difference*, which started life as one thing and finished as another, this idea for a history of the Liffey bridges in the order of their construction has been nagging away in my head for years. Well, it's done now for better or worse. I hope that the intention that lay behind the idea – that such a survey might prove to be a new and original way of tracing the development of Ireland's capital city – has been realised.

A City Runs Through Them could not have been attempted, let alone written, without the work of a generation or more of outstanding scholars who have done so much to recover Dublin's past. Their work is acknowledged both in the source references studded through the text and in the bibliography. In this connection, I must single out the late J.W. De Courcy's *The Liffey in Dublin* as an exemplary work of scholarship. I know of no other work, on this subject or any other, so scrupulous, reliable and abundant.

I am of course grateful to those friends and colleagues who read and reviewed the text in draft and supplied helpful comments. They include Angela Long, Michael Fewer, Jonathan Williams,

Sandra D'Arcy and Pat Cooke. It is hardly necessary to say that any and all remaining errors, omissions and other *bêtises* in the body of the text are their fault. I take the Nixon defence: I accept responsibility, but not the blame.

As before, I am grateful to the staff at Atlantic Books for the faith they have shown in the book. Will Atkinson as publisher and James Nightingale as senior editor have been vital supports as well as sure-footed professional advisers.

A HISTORY OF THE
CITY IN 362 WORDS

DUBLIN BEGAN AS a Viking trading settlement in the middle of the tenth century. Location was key to its quick ascendancy among Irish towns. It commanded the shortest crossing to a major port in Britain. By the time the Normans arrived in the late twelfth century, this was crucial: Dublin maintained the best communications between the English crown and its new lordship in Ireland.

The city first developed on the rising ground south of the river where Christ Church now stands. The English established their principal citadel, Dublin Castle, in this area. Throughout the medieval and early modern periods, the town's importance was largely ecclesiastical and strategic. It was neither a centre of learning nor fashion, and its commerce was modest.

The foundation of Trinity College in 1592 was a landmark event but the town did not begin to turn into a city until after the restoration of Charles II in 1660 and the arrival of the Duke of Ormond as his viceroy. The final victory of the Protestant colonial interest in Ireland ushered in the long peace of the eighteenth century. Then a series of fine, wide Georgian streets, squares and noble public buildings appeared, Dublin's greatest boast. A semi-autonomous parliament of the Anglo-Irish creoles provided a focus for social life. The city prospered.

This parliament dissolved itself in 1800 under the terms of the Act of Union, and Ireland became a full part of the British metropolitan state, a situation not reversed until Irish independence in 1922 (Northern Ireland always excepted). The union years saw Dublin decline. Fine old town houses were gradually abandoned by the aristocracy – increasingly absent – and became hideous tenement warrens. The city missed out on the industrial revolution. Its commercial middle class migrated to new suburbs beyond the two canals.

Independence restored some of its natural function but there was still much poverty and shabbiness. The 1960s mini-boom was a false dawn. Only since the 1990s has there been real evidence of a city reinventing and revitalising itself. The 2008 economic crash was a form of cardiac arrest, leaving many unresolved problems. There is still much to be done.

A CITY RUNS THROUGH THEM

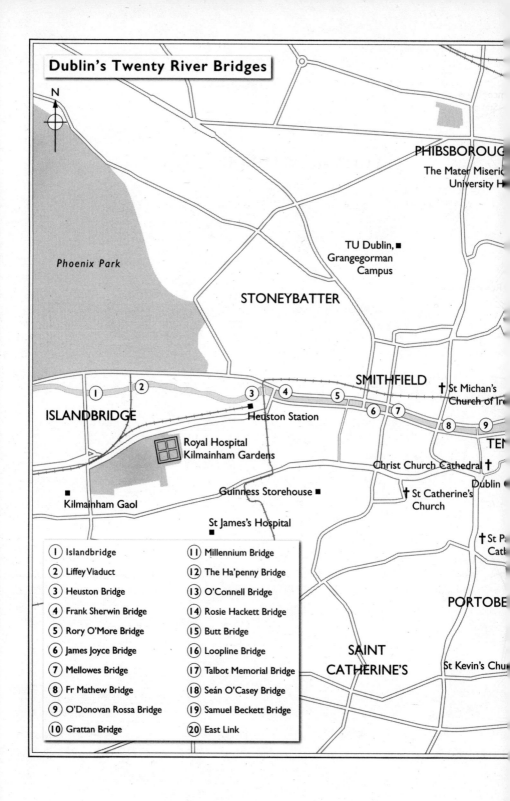

Dublin's Twenty River Bridges

N

Phoenix Park

PHIBSBOROUG

The Mater Miseric
University H

TU Dublin, ■
Grangegorman
Campus

STONEYBATTER

SMITHFIELD   † St Michan's
Church of Ire

ISLANDBRIDGE

Heuston Station

Royal Hospital
Kilmainham Gardens

Christ Church Cathedral †

Dublin (

TEI

Kilmainham Gaol

Guinness Storehouse ■

† St Catherine's
Church

St James's Hospital

† St P.
Catl

PORTOBE

SAINT
CATHERINE'S

St Kevin's Chur

(1) Islandbridge
(2) Liffey Viaduct
(3) Heuston Bridge
(4) Frank Sherwin Bridge
(5) Rory O'More Bridge
(6) James Joyce Bridge
(7) Mellowes Bridge
(8) Fr Mathew Bridge
(9) O'Donovan Rossa Bridge
(10) Grattan Bridge

(11) Millennium Bridge
(12) The Ha'penny Bridge
(13) O'Connell Bridge
(14) Rosie Hackett Bridge
(15) Butt Bridge
(16) Loopline Bridge
(17) Talbot Memorial Bridge
(18) Seán O'Casey Bridge
(19) Samuel Beckett Bridge
(20) East Link

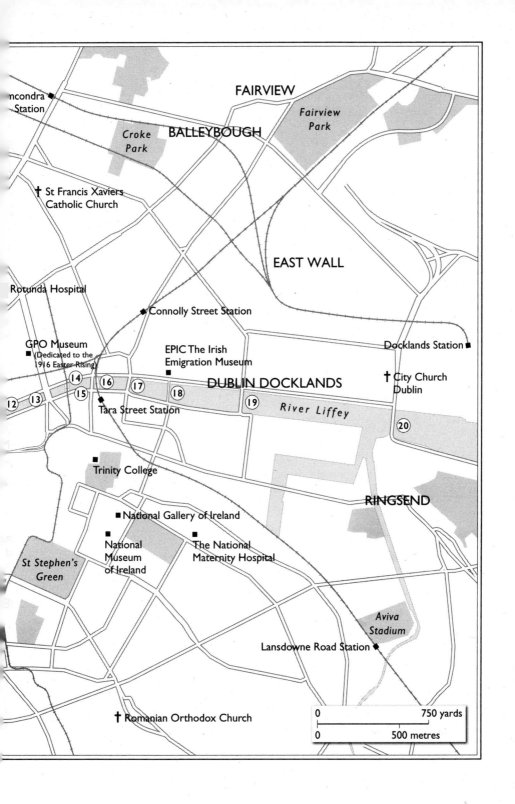

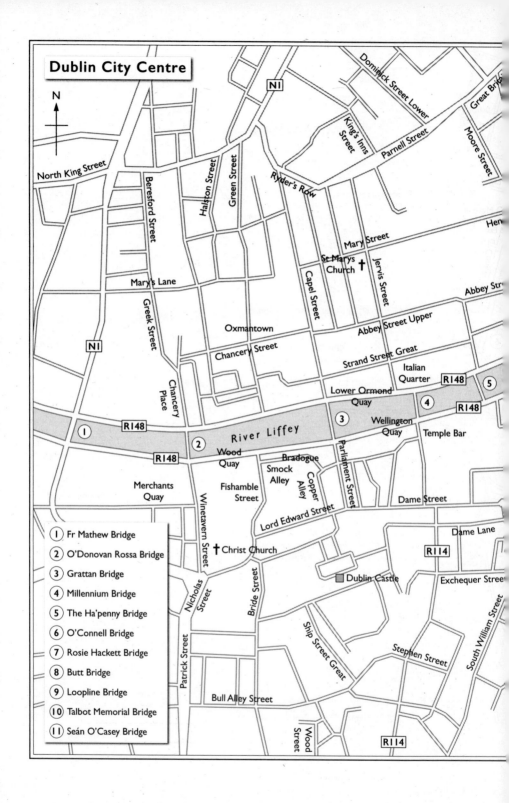

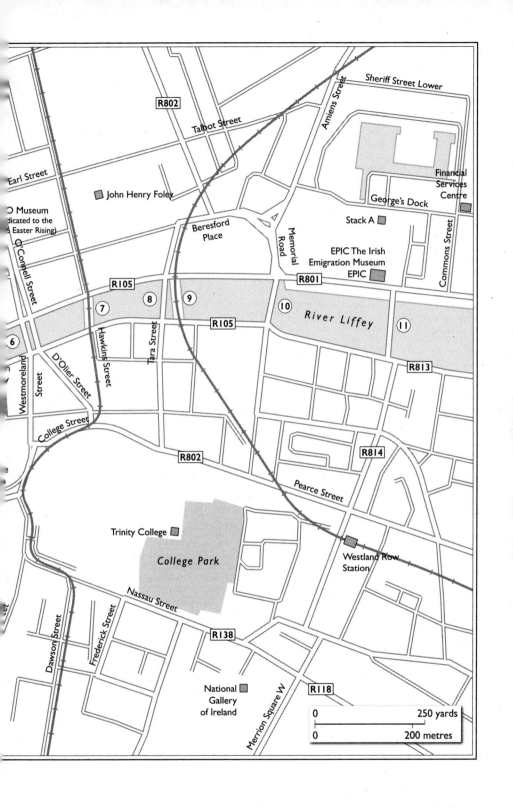

INTRODUCTION

THERE ARE MANY ways of telling a city's history. Few things that have happened have happened entirely by accident or chance. Most are deliberate, and there is hardly a human action more deliberate than throwing a bridge across water. That is especially so in cities with well-articulated quarters on either bank, as in Paris or London or, on a more modest scale, Dublin. There are rivers in cities like Edinburgh or Brussels that you might miss completely, so tucked away are they. There are cities like Turin or Vienna where the substantial part of the city is on one bank only. There are places with no rivers at all.

Dublin started life on the south bank of the Liffey, on the rising ground that runs up to Christ Church. That rising ground is in fact a geological ridge that runs east–west parallel to the river and offers strategic control over its tidal reaches. And for six or seven centuries, that is more or less where the town stayed, with just a nervous north-side suburb in nearby St Michan's parish: Oxmantown. Until the 1660s Dublin was at first little more than a village, then a town of some little consequence, but still small as such places go, in comparative terms, and still hugging the area around that ridge of rising ground that runs east from Kilmainham to what is now the west end of Dame Street.

In all that time, there was only one bridge over the urban Liffey. There was no need for more, there being so little on the far side. Then suddenly, in the space of fewer than twenty years after 1670, three more bridges were thrown up and the north side was born. (There were actually four, but one was soon destroyed in a flood and not rebuilt.) A process was begun that might be described as northing and easting. As the modern city formed, it did so by twin impulses: developing what had hitherto been open fields north of the river while simultaneously – albeit gradually but inexorably – pushing east towards the bay.

The purpose of this book is to trace the process by looking at these various river crossings chronologically, in the order of their construction. I begin this book as I shall finish it, deficient in knowledge of civil engineering. So how these bridges were actually constructed and made safe is less my subject than the municipal and political motivation behind these structures and the effect that each one had on its hinterland on either side of the river. From this patchwork quilt I hope to construct an impressionistic history of the city. It can be little more than that, for you will learn little here of the far-flung suburbs, remote from the river. What you may learn, however, is how the musculature of the city developed and how it determined the shape and purpose of the modern urban space.

Every Dubliner knows about north-side–south-side jokes: well, without the bridges there wouldn't be any. The contrary theme of east and west may seem less obvious but is, in my view, more potent sociologically, as I hope the following pages demonstrate. Without that process of northing and easting, for instance, there would be no trace of that postal district and state of mind known as Dublin 4, the *locus classicus* of bourgeois amour propre – which would be an intolerable absence.

The book, therefore, does not follow the flow of the river from Islandbridge to the sea. Instead, it hops back and forth according to the construction dates of the bridges themselves. So this is jigsaw history: until all the awkward pieces have been properly placed, the overall picture remains unclear.

What is undeniable, though, is the extraordinary momentum that the bridges provided to the city's sudden and precocious development. Prior to 1660, Dublin is an inconsequential little provincial town in an out-of-the-way location. Within a century, it is being talked of as one of the ten largest cities *in Europe*. Of course, much of that is speculation, as there was no certain way of counting people in a pre-censual age, although measuring urban footprint presented fewer difficulties. But population estimates can hardly have been so inaccurate or inflated as to be completely false. Who can say with certainty that Dublin was bigger or smaller than Naples or Madrid in 1780? But the mere fact that it was being discussed in the same breath as these great royal and imperial centres marked its advance from the margins of urban consciousness towards the centre. These estimates of comparative size, while never absolutely definitive, are generally accepted as roughly accurate by most modern scholars.

It might have happened otherwise. Who is to say? Dublin could have stayed on one side of the river, like Turin, and pushed south. But it didn't. It went north, and in due time it swarmed all over the place. And without the bridges, none of that would have happened. Something else inscrutable might have quickened, and for all anyone knows, Terenure today might be regarded as the

Boulevard Saint-Michel or the Upper East Side. But to the relief of many, that's not how it all panned out.

––––––

Obviously, not all bridges are equal. While it is the purpose of this book to trace each one and its effect on the geographical and historical development of the city, some were obviously more critical to the Dublin that has actually evolved from the series of accidents, plans and contingencies that constitute any historical process.

The two bridges that I think have mattered most to the development of the modern city – the one we actually know in the twenty-first century – are Capel Street Bridge and O'Connell Bridge. Incidentally, for most of what follows in this book, I avoid as far as I can the 'official' names of bridges, which names have been subject to change over time. British ruling worthies, viceroys and their lady wives generally got bridges (and other items of public furniture) named for them. Unsurprisingly, that habit passed out of fashion at independence, and the bridges, like the mainline railway stations, were generally renamed for persons distinguished in the radical nationalist tradition. In one case, Rosie Hackett, the choice remains original and is a nod both to feminism and to the labour movement; in three others, literature is acknowledged in the persons of Joyce, Beckett and O'Casey. But in general the patriots scooped the pool.

Not that it was especially helpful in identifying which bridge was which. Most Dubliners would find it hard to tell you which one was Rory O'More Bridge – I could not have told you offhand before I began working on this book – and might prefer Watling Street Bridge, although even there many would remain a bit vague.

Old-timers called it Bloody Bridge, the name that had the longest shelf life and the one that Joyce uses in *Ulysses*. But as we shall see, it was renamed for O'More.

Something similar, although not as stark, applies to one of the two most consequential bridges. Which one is Grattan Bridge? Some Dubs might struggle, or at least hesitate. And what was it originally? Ah yes, Essex Bridge – named for the viceroy whose patronage enabled it. Essex was his honorific; his family name was Capel, thus the name of the street that runs off it to the north. So calling it Capel Street Bridge, which most people do, makes everything clear, while official nomenclature, both anachronistic and modern, only causes degrees of confusion.

On the other hand, there is absolutely no confusion about which one is O'Connell Bridge (although in the old days it was Carlisle Bridge, named for yet another viceroy, as was the street that gave on to it from the north side, Sackville Street: what a well-mannered, deferential lot we were, never done tipping our caps to the quality). The bridge was not renamed for Daniel O'Connell until 1880 and the street not until as late as 1924. But even when they were Sackville Street and Carlisle Bridge, nobody was unsure of their location. Not so, as we have seen and will see later in some more detail, with the post-independence renamings.

Of all the twenty bridges covered in what follows, these two – at Capel Street and at the southern end of O'Connell Street – are the two that more than any others changed the entire orientation of the city.

It will be elaborated on in the book but it bears mentioning here in summary form. Prior to the building of Capel Street Bridge, the north side barely existed. Speed's map of 1610 is our best guide in this. Across the river from the little town on the

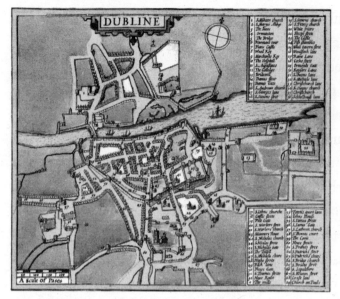

John Speed's *Dubline* is the oldest surviving map of the city, published in 1611

south side, huddling around Christ Church Cathedral, although by now well spread beyond the small embracing walls, there was only a scatter of habitation.

The big thing that had been over there – St Mary's Abbey, established as a Cistercian foundation around 1147, having previously been a Savignac house for a few years and possibly a Benedictine one as early as 968[1] – had been razed in the state-sponsored vandalism known as the dissolution of the monasteries in the late 1530s. It was a substantial complex, whose sister house was Buildwas Abbey in Shropshire.

Yet that earlier dissolution of monastic and other religious establishments, with its incalculable artistic losses at the hands of fanatics, was a moment of caesura. Nothing much happened in urban development that can engage the historical memory for the next hundred years or so, but when things started to happen, they happened in a rush. This was in the 1670s and '80s, when suddenly four new bridges were thrown across the urban river where hitherto there had only been one. Of these four, Capel Street Bridge was not the first – that distinction belongs to O'More/Bloody/Watling Street Bridge a bit upriver – none the less it was by far the most transformative.

As we shall see in chapter 4, the effect of building this bridge was to open up and urbanise the north shore of the river. It was filled in and developed in a remarkably short period of time, considering the inertia antecedent. It was not alone in this: as we'll see in chapter 3, O'More Bridge was material in this respect as well, as were all the other bridges thrown up at this time. But none were as decisive in turning Dublin from a huddling little trading town on one side of the Liffey only to a proper two-sided city as we have come to know it. Look at Charles Brooking's map of 1728 – not much more than a century after Speed's – and you are hard pressed to believe you are looking at a rendering of the same place. The early north side is full.

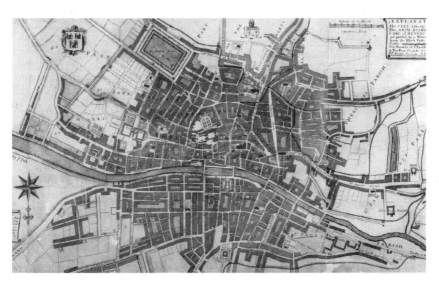

Dublin's north side developed exponentially in the century between Speed's and Brooking's maps

Moreover, the river is progressively contained. The original embanking went back to Dublin's earliest days, but it was only with the sudden growth of the burgeoning town that the process became urgent and continuous, so that the North Wall – running all the way down to what is now the East Link Bridge – was in place as early as the first decades of the eighteenth century, although constantly in need of updating and repair until it reached its modern state around 1840. Look at any of the old maps of the town, say pre-Brooking, to see how ragged was the natural course of the Liffey, all little indents, pools and irregularities. The quay walls imposed a sort of Enlightenment order on this undisciplined state of nature. Before it was anything else, Dublin was a harbour town. Its life blood was marine commerce; therefore, that commerce, as it expanded, required engineering infrastructure even that far downriver, well away from the town, to sustain itself.

It is ironic that Dublin's classical age – the Georgian period, to employ a shorthand that is almost accurate – should have been born on the north side and most of its early heroic architectural achievements located there, considering the sad shambles into which so much of it has been allowed to fall in modern times. That's for a later plaint in the body of the book. But it makes the point that without the north side the Dublin that we actually know is literally unimaginable. Capel Street and O'Connell Street as undeveloped green fields, anyone?

———

The manner in which the story that follows is told tells us something about Dublin. This question of using the Liffey bridges as the prompt or the hinge on which the historical development of the city is hung is only possible for a small city, and one with not too many bridges. And Dublin, for all its occasional bouts of self-congratulation – which are fair enough: no one should be ashamed to cheer for their team – is a small city. It is a small city, but one with a very large footprint for its population. This low-density sprawl makes it difficult to facilitate an excellent, integrated and efficient public transport system.

You couldn't write a book like this for London or Paris. London is just too vast; Paris has a ridiculous number of bridges. In London, it would not be difficult to write sensibly about Westminster Bridge and to identify its contribution to the history of the city. Likewise London Bridge, obviously, or Waterloo Bridge. But Chiswick Bridge or even Kew Bridge? By the time you'd got from Teddington – the tidal reach of the Thames – down to Tower Bridge, you'd have a baggy, incoherent book. As for Paris, don't even think of it.

But it's manageable for Dublin, even allowing that all twenty bridges are not equal in their historical significance and – to be fair – some are of minimal significance, if even that. I have tried to reflect these inequalities in the text. But in the cases of the bridges that have the greatest importance, their contribution to how the city actually developed has been crucial. Once more, the most obvious examples are Capel Street Bridge and O'Connell Bridge, for the reasons set out earlier in this introduction. There is, however, something to say about all of them.

So: time to cross that bridge now that we have come to it.

– ❀ –

ONE

FR MATHEW BRIDGE

THE BRIDGE ON this site was, until 1670, the only urban river crossing on the Liffey. It lies just to the west of the Four Courts, upstream a little from the old walled Viking and early Norman town. It stands at or very close to *Áth Cliath*, the ford of the hurdles. This was a fording place across the river at low tide: the hurdles refer to what is supposed to be a series of timber mattings that gave pedestrians a degree of grip as they made their way across. This ford gave the town that grew up beside it its name in the Irish language: *Baile Átha Cliath*, or the town of the ford of hurdles.

It was not without occasional danger. The annals record a catastrophic event in 770 when an army, apparently returning from a victory and perhaps flushed with alcohol, was caught by a sudden incoming tide: many were drowned. This is a reminder that the entire stretch of the Liffey covered in this book is tidal, from Islandbridge at the western margin to the point where it empties into the bay below the East Link Bridge. And Dublin Bay is tidal, very. The tidal rhythm basically occupies about six hours each day, giving two high and two low tides in any twenty-four hours. On the day I type this, the difference in height between the first high and the first low tide is 2.15 metres or (in old money) 7.05 feet, a fairly typical tidal range, although it can on occasion go as high as 3 metres. So, eastward on the river estuary the tide is full and generous when flowing but leaves a rather desolate sandscape – with orphaned pools of water here and there – when fully out.

That desolate scenario is repeated upriver at low tide, so that even today, with the river firmly embanked at Fr Mathew Bridge, it is hard not to conclude that the troops who drowned in 770 were either reckless or unlucky, or perhaps both. Did they decide to take their chance against a fast-flowing tide? It's hard to account otherwise for what actually happened, fuelled perhaps by drink and victors' bravado. Of course, the river was not embanked in those days and flowed unimpeded in its natural channel, making it both wider and shallower at this point. At any rate, this incident, for which the annalistic evidence appears reliable, is a reminder that, hurdles or no hurdles, the fording point was not free of hazard.

But why was there a ford here at all? After all, there was no town nearby, not yet, nor would there be the beginnings of one for the best part of another two hundred years. And for six centuries and more after its modest foundation by the Vikings in the late tenth century, it was a place of little consequence in the great affairs of the world. So why was there a ford here?

Look seaward, then landward. This was obviously a site of some importance. All the later significance attached to Dublin derived from its marine approaches. Its bay is the only great, dramatic opening for shipping on the east coast of Ireland. The Boyne, just over forty kilometres north of the Liffey, has no such reception room. Although its valley for some distance inland has been settled since Neolithic times, the river enters the sea at Mornington in a manner that is best described as apologetic. Dublin Bay, on the other hand, is a fabulously extravagant marine drawing room that bids you in.

The ford was where it was not because of the sea or the river, but because of the roads to landward. This was the point at which four major roads from the Irish interior converged. Why here? There was no town, no settlement, nothing permanent. Intelligent inference is the best that can serve. These internal roads led towards Dublin Bay to facilitate commerce with Roman and later with Anglo-Saxon England, for which the bay provided a point of goods inwards and outwards. It opened the shortest sea route to the rich midlands and south of England for the trading of whatever there was to trade. In Roman times, the principal connection was with the fortified town of *Deva Victrix*, a Roman fort (*castrum*) from which it takes its modern name, Chester. A sufficient number of Roman artefacts have been discovered at Irish archaeological sites to render a Roman commercial presence in Ireland beyond dispute.

The ancient roads that converged on Dublin ran through flat country, giving easy access both ways. The one exception was the *Slí Cualann*, coming from South Leinster and the Waterford region. It encountered the natural barrier of the Wicklow Mountains, immediately south of the modern city. But even there, while it was difficult to go through the mountains, it was perfectly possible to go round them. There was a coastal littoral to the east which offered one option; moreover, to the west the mountains quickly fell away down to the plains of Kildare. All in all, the road system offered easy access from Dublin Bay to the interior, and it offered the interior easy access to Dublin Bay.

An archaeological illustrator's impression of the hurdled ford

So, from ancient times, before we have any secure written records that mark the beginnings of history proper, there is sufficient circumstantial and archaeological evidence to suggest that the Dublin Bay area was some sort of a trading entrepôt. There is no evidence of any permanent settlement until the arrival of the Vikings in the late eighth century, but again it would not be wholly unreasonable to suppose that there may have been seasonal trading camps in the area from time to time.

So who laid the hurdles that formed *Áth Cliath*? The hurdles amounted to a matting of latticed timbers secured to the river bottom by some means or other. That suggests something more than a temporary gimcrack, which in *its* turn suggests some sort of regular – if not actually permanent – human presence. If the fording point was, on this speculation, a commercial pinch point, it was in the interest of those traders and merchants who functioned there to maintain it in a state of regular good order.

Nor was it all ford. The site chosen for the crossing also contained an island in the river. This was Usher's Island, long since gone as a physical feature, but very handy in the long ago. It survives vestigially in the name of one of Dublin's south quays, opposite where it once stood (see chapter 17). It would have made every sense to have taken advantage of such a fortuitous feature in selecting the site of the ford. So, in aggregate, a number of factors combined to make this the remote spot near which would later cluster the early permanent Viking settlements that were the physical beginnings of Dublin: the converging roads; the convenient ford; the ready access to the bay for commerce.

Its natural position combined with human activity marked it out as the site of the island's principal town from the beginning. The many Irish marine raids on Roman Britain – one of which produced St Patrick – had been a consistent feature of the early centuries AD. Many must have launched from Dublin Bay. It is not easy to imagine where piracy stopped and trade began, that is supposing that they could be segregated at all and were not part of a common, tangled warlord system. We don't know what was traded either way, although it is likely that Irish volunteers for the Roman army were a feature; that would have been consistent with ordinary Roman practice on other margins of the empire. We don't know for certain if slaves were traded, as they were to be in Viking times to come, but it is a reasonable speculation. The entire ancient world depended on forced labour: slaves were an irreplaceable part of every ancient economy and society, without which none could have functioned. No slaves, no Aristotle.

The coming of Christianity to Ireland in the fifth century AD resulted in the development of many monastic sites. In fact, monastic organisation was to remain the defining feature of the Irish Christian Church for centuries. In this, it echoed other church organisational structures at the margins of early Christianity, where Roman influence had been weak or non-existent: the Coptic Church of Upper Egypt and Ethiopia is a good example, as are the wilds of Arabia Deserta with its famous monastery of St Catherine.

However, and here's a crucial difference, in the post-Roman heartland of Latin Christianity, roughly co-terminus with the nerve centre of Charlemagne's empire astride the Rhine, ecclesiastical organisation was diocesan. Each diocese was based on a town; such towns were a necklace of commercial and military settlements of Roman origin that survived the collapse of the empire and then furnished the musculature of the diocesan system of church organisation.

Ireland, having no towns, had not the means to establish dioceses along continental lines, so the monasteries filled the gap. The first monastery along the Liffey of which we have solid knowledge dates from the seventh century and was situated downstream of *Átha Cliath*, at the eastern end of the long gravel ridge running in from Kilmainham, just before it falls away towards the top of what is now Dame Street. The site is now occupied by Dublin Castle. In the seventh century, it had the advantage of both height – thanks to the ridge – and the presence of water on three sides: the Liffey itself at the front and the Poddle – long since culverted – wrapping round to the south and east as it approached its confluence with the bigger river. In particular, the Poddle formed a tidal pool later named in Irish as *Dubh Linn*, the dark pool. This was anglicised in due course as Dublin and gave the city its name in the English language. The fact that *Dubh Linn and Átha Cliath* were different settlements, albeit contiguous, accounts for the linguistic difference in the Irish and the English names of the modern city. The Irish form of the earlier settlement stuck, as did the anglicised form of the latter.

Then the Vikings came.

The early Scandinavian settlement, on the rising ground that ran up from the river to the gravel ridge, was protected by earthen defences. But as the little town acquired a sense of permanence, stone wall defences were built. The earliest are estimated to date to about 1100 and were later augmented and extended in stone by the Normans. The Vikings also threw the first bridge across the Liffey. It was built just beside *Átha Cliath* – that is, just west and upstream of the walled town itself.

Why there? On the face of it, it would surely have made more sense to connect the settlement directly to the north bank from what is now the end of Winetavern Street, within the walls, on the line of what is now O'Donovan Rossa Bridge (although no one calls it that; it is simply Winetavern Street Bridge to most Dubliners). But to do that might have been to weaken the defences of the town. After all, a bridge can be crossed from either end; had the bridge been built there, it would probably have necessitated a defensive barbican on the south side, which may have been beyond the engineering or financial capacity of the potential defenders. Just as likely, perhaps even more so, is the significance of that proximity to *Átha Cliath*, because that marked the point at which the *Slí Midluachra*, one of the four principal roads of ancient Ireland, met the Liffey and by extension the sea. This road ran along the east coast from south Ulster. Its position seems to have accounted for the location of the ford of *Átha Cliath* – likewise, on the same principle, of the bridge.

So they built their bridge here, a bit upstream of the walled town and beside the old ford. No one knows the foundation date, but a wooden structure appears to have been in position by 1000. The other advantage of this location was that it either opened up or gave access to a pre-existing Norse suburb on the north bank. This was Oxmantown – the town of the Ostmen or east men – which was sufficiently well-established by the late eleventh century to merit its own parish church, St Michan's. It is no accident that this very first bridge over the Liffey opened up or gave access to a northern suburb. This is precisely what happened on a much grander scale when Dublin bridge-building really took off six hundred years later, in the 1670s and '80s.

Oxmantown grew in extent after the arrival of the Normans to the city in 1170. As the newcomers began to dominate and bully the existing population of the walled town, many found it expedient to cluster on the north side among their own people, a kind of voluntary ghetto. Indeed, the bridge was referred to in the thirteenth century as Ostmans Bridge, merely one of the myriad names it has had over the years.

This was to be the only bridge over the urban Liffey until 1670. Even then, it was not always there. Although rebuilt at the time of King John in 1214 to replace the old Viking structure, it was dismantled in 1316 and its materials used to strengthen the town's defences against an anticipated attack by the forces of Edward Bruce – Robert the Bruce's brother – who had invaded Ireland with the intention of setting up an independent kingdom there. That danger passed and the bridge was rebuilt only to be destroyed by flood waters in 1385. The town decided that it could do so well without it that it was not rebuilt for over forty years, until 1428. But from that date, there has always been a bridge on this site.

It has had many names at different times, including Dublin Bridge – thus echoing London Bridge when that was the only bridge across the Thames. The 1428 structure survived, in various states of repair and disrepair, until it was replaced by the present structure in 1818. It had long been acknowledged that the old bridge had been in ever-deteriorating condition, and it was clear that sooner or later it would have to be replaced. The wonder is that it took as long as it did, because doubts about its safety were voiced as early as the turn of the seventeenth century. So it took more than two hundred years of prevaricating and patching up before the current structure was erected.

It was renamed yet again, this time as Whitworth Bridge, to acknowledge Charles, Lord Whitworth, who was lord lieutenant (or viceroy) at the time. He also had a suburban road in Drumcondra named for him, running along the north bank of

Engraving showing the River Liffey, with the Four Courts and Whitworth Bridge

the Royal Canal, onto whose southern bank projects the boundary of Mountjoy Prison, opened in 1850; it was here that, years later, Brendan Behan, then serving time for membership of the IRA, heard the ringing of the warden's triangle to waken the prisoners each morning: 'and the ould triangle went jingle jangle / all along the banks of the Royal Canal'. Whitworth Road has retained its viceregal name to this day, which is more than can be said of the bridge.

In 1922, on the establishment of the Irish Free State, it was decided to revert to the simple name of Dublin Bridge. That didn't last long. In 1938, its name was changed again to honour Fr Theobald Mathew (1790–1856), the great mid-nineteenth-century temperance campaigner. In 1838, he himself took a pledge of total abstinence, saying 'here goes in the name of the Lord'. He then began a public campaign to wean Ireland off the ravages of alcohol, using the slogan 'Ireland sober is Ireland free'. This echoed the contemporary nationalist campaigns of Daniel O'Connell.

Fr Mathew's campaign was an astonishing success, so much so that in the six years up to the outbreak of the Famine in 1845, the revenues raised in Ireland from the sale of spirits fell by nearly 50 per cent.

His successful trespass into this alcoholic territory was impressive by any standard. Ireland lived down to its own caricature: it had an enormous problem with alcohol, not least illicit alcohol. Illegal hootch – poitín – was rife. In south Ulster, ether-drinking was common. Ether, which is a distillate of alcohol treated with sulphuric acid, is required to be adulterated to make it tolerable for human consumption; the adulterate was usually poitín. It was very effective and gave the drinker a tremendous high.

It was a problem that could be contained and ameliorated

for a while, but like a dormant volcano it had a nasty habit of re-emerging. By the end of the nineteenth century, with Fr Mathew long in his grave, another priest – Fr James Cullen SJ – felt the need to found the Pioneer Total Abstinence Association, once again to combat the revival of the demon drink. As with Fr Mathew's campaign, it was hugely successful, and for years it was commonplace to see men's jacket lapels bearing the Sacred Heart insignia which was the Pioneers' symbol.

Along with other ostentatiously Catholic causes, its best years were those of the mid-twentieth-century Catholic hegemony, from which the latter-day Irish are now fleeing headlong in secular embarrassment. You'd be pushed to see a Pioneer pin on any lapel these days: it's seriously uncool. But as recently as the 1950s – that is, within living memory, just – the Pioneers numbered almost half a million people out of a population of just under three million. However, by the early twenty-first century it was back to business as usual. According to the World Atlas, Ireland was seventh in the world in alcohol consumption in 2017, measured in litres per capita. That doesn't sound too bad until you see the countries that are above it: Estonia, Belarus, Lithuania, Andorra, the Czech Republic and Austria. So ignoring Andorra – too small to be statistically relevant – Ireland has the second-highest consumption rate among countries that never suffered from prolonged Soviet occupation.

Fr Mathew and his clerical successors may, therefore, be regarded as Sisyphean, condemned to an endlessly virtuous futility. You can appreciate why the old bridge was finally named for him. He was important in himself as the progenitor of a huge and significant social movement and, in particular, one so heavily associated with a public projection of Catholic virtue in a hyper-

Catholic era. Not that it has done much to enhance his historical memory: most Dubliners couldn't tell you where Fr Mathew Bridge is. To them, and to all of us, it's simply Church Street Bridge and there's an end of it.

This is fair enough, for Church Street – named for the church of St Michan, which dates from the 1090s – has a fair claim to be the oldest established Dublin street outside the walls. Here, in Oxmantown, was Dublin's first north-side suburb. It is clear from John Speed's map of 1610 that Oxmantown is well developed, if sparsely in comparison with the walled town south of the river. In the course of time, this suburb would push north along the line of Church Street to embrace Broadstone and Phibsborough up as far as the Royal Canal at the top of Whitworth Road. That was all to come later, in the eighteenth century, as Rocque's great city atlas of 1756 testifies. Speed's map is invaluable, however, because it shows the town while it was still a town, before the heroic period of development that began in the 1660s and turned it into the city mapped by Rocque and his successors.

The general point is plain and will, I fear, be repeated quite often in this book, if only because the ineluctable logic of geography proposes repetition: without the bridges, there is no north side, or nothing much worth mentioning. The entire physical development of Dublin – what I referred to in the introduction as the process of northing and easting that turned the town into a city – depends almost completely on the various bridges that are the subject of this study. No bridges, no north side. No north side, no city.

The north side of the river had every advantage for development, most of all rising ground. Much of the land to the south-east of the walled town – the part that eventually ended up as the centre of fashion and desire – was low lying and swampy. But north of the river was all uphill, well above any flood line. And, indeed, once extra-mural development began, it began to the north, across the river. Wealth likes an eminence and could find it here. But even on the north side, development was more focused on the north-east rather than the north-west quadrant, despite the latter having the temporal advantage of Church Street, the longest established main drag. A telling detail in this regard is that in the 1830s almost 900 solicitors – out of a total of about 1,500 – were living in the new north-east residential streets centred on Mountjoy Square. Very few were living west of Capel Street, despite the presence of the Four Courts there. A similar pattern applied to barristers: by 1836, more than a quarter of those who had taken silk were living in Merrion Square, no less – the finest address in the city and even more remote from the Four Courts.[1]

Church Street led north to Broadstone and to Phibsborough – both developed from the eighteenth century on. It grew to include buildings of distinction – the Blue Coat School, the King's Inns, Broadstone rail terminus, some churches of modest but definite architectural accomplishment – but it never established itself as a centre of fashion. As we shall see in due course, the process of northing and easting created a sort of fashionable crescent, sweeping in time first from the north-east quadrant and then across the river to the great squares and gardens of the south-east: Merrion, Fitzwilliam and St Stephen's Green.

All of this left the north-west quadrant, centred on Church Street and its later extensions, something of a fashion orphan. And so it has remained until recently, when a gradual process of gentrification has brought forth a solid extension of bourgeois professionals into the area around Stoneybatter and Manor Street (see chapter 17). Even at that, the city authorities' ambitious attempt to create a new civic centre based on the long rectangular open space of Smithfield has not been a success – without being an outright failure.

The city just does not want to move west, or at least its beating heart does not. In reality, the western suburbs beyond the Phoenix Park are a vast and depressing sprawl for the most part. It may be populous but the energy and the force is not there, out in the nondescript housing estates either side of the upper Liffey valley.

Yet it is none the less to the west that we turn next. The earlier statement that there was only one bridge over the river until 1670 is only half-true. It is absolutely true of the urban core. But a few kilometres upstream, near the river's tidal reach at Islandbridge, there was, as the name suggests, a bridge. The first version of it dates from 1577 and it is to it, to its successor structure and to its fascinating neighbourhood that we next direct our attention.

– ✿ –

TWO

ISLANDBRIDGE

THE WHOLE INTERPRETATIVE thrust of this book has to do with the process of northing and easting. Thus Dublin grows from a town to a city by expansion from the central southern core around Christ Church across the Liffey to the north side. That's where it first establishes its city credentials, mainly in the north-east quadrant, before sweeping back across the river to settle the south-east quadrant, which remains to this day the principal locus of fashion and display.

So what are we doing, so early in the telling of all this, by going in the opposite direction? No northing and easting here, just westing. Islandbridge lies upstream, at the river's tidal reach, and it is here that the second bridge ever thrown across the Liffey was built in 1577, a century before the huge bridge-building expansion downriver that facilitated the northing and easting process. So this is something of an historical cul-de-sac in terms of my overall narrative.

None the less, since my purpose is to trace the development of Dublin through the chronological order of its bridges, I must embrace the anomaly and do what I can to explain it and see how it can fit into a general pattern to which it is clearly exceptional. Otherwise, I'd be like a horse that falls at the first fence in the Grand National.

That phrase 'tidal reach' offers us the best clue. There is something numinous about that point in a riverine journey where suddenly it is gripped by the mysterious force of tidal currents. It marks a change of character: it has now acquired this additional power, linking it directly to the great sea beyond – and the entire process superintended by the phases of the moon. It is not hard to understand how earlier people, who as yet had no understanding of these natural forces, could invest this moment with religious reverence and awe.

Even in modern times, with all that understanding available to us, it is an image that has inspired rhapsody. Consider this passage from MacNeice's *Autumn Journal*, fourth canto, in which he apostrophises his lover Nancy Coldstream:

So I am glad
That life contains her with her moods and moments
More shifting and more transient than I had
Yet thought of as being integral to beauty;
Whose mind is like the wind on a sea of wheat,
Whose eyes are candour,
And assurance in her feet
Like a homing pigeon never by doubt diverted.
To whom I send my thanks
That the air has become shot silk, the streets are music,
And that the ranks
Of men are ranks of men, no more of cyphers.

So that if now alone
I must pursue this life, it will not be only
A drag from stone to numbered stone
But a ladder of angels, river turning tidal.

And it is perhaps that sense of numinous awe that explains why this relatively overlooked part of inner west Dublin was in fact settled from ancient times.

It is almost impossible to discuss Islandbridge without mentioning Kilmainham, which stands up the hill to the south of the river, astride the same gravel ridge on which the early Viking town downstream was centred. That command of rising ground gave Kilmainham the same defensive advantage that it was to give to the Viking town. There was a monastery there from as early as the seventh century. Invariably, any such institution in its turn attracted secular proto-villages adjacent. The monastery itself did not survive the depredations of the Vikings and it vanished from history long before AD 1000. Down the hill, at Islandbridge, there was a ford at the tidal reach.

The sudden, brutal arrival of the Vikings in the late eighth century was one of the most consequential events in all of Irish history. They were raiders and traders but, critically, they were town builders. They founded the early medieval town of Dublin, on the hill where Christ Church Cathedral stands today at the eastern end of the gravel ridge, drawing their longboats up on the sandy shore of the Liffey's south bank. But they also pushed further upriver, towards the tidal reach at Islandbridge, where they were also able to beach their boats.

That gave them the access to Kilmainham that put an end to the monastery. Monasteries were an easy and tempting target for these raiders, being conspicuous centres of wealth and therefore obvious targets for plunder. There may even have been a small satellite Viking settlement in the vicinity of Islandbridge/ Kilmainham in the ninth century, because a Viking burial ground has been discovered there by archaeologists. But there is no certain evidence of any such settlement. There is no doubt about the burials, however, which are recognisably Viking in character. For example, bodies were buried with grave goods, a practice forbidden by Christian usage. The burial ground echoes features found at other Viking funerary sites in the general vicinity of Dublin.

The monastery up the hill at Kilmainham was eventually reconstituted, and by the early thirteenth century its monks had created a weir at Islandbridge. To do this, they dammed the river and created a mill race. This formed the island that gave the place its name. It is speculated, and highly probable, that there was a bridge here from the thirteenth century, but we can't be at all sure of this. What we can be sure of is that there was built a real bridge

An eighteenth-century prospect of Dublin as seen from Magazine Hill in Phoenix Park

in 1577, under the direction of the lord deputy Sir Henry Sidney – whatever speculative structure may have been there antecedent, Sidney's bridge was made of stone. This is, apart from the bridge at Church Street downriver, the first solid structure across the Liffey of which we have certain knowledge.

The obvious questions are: why build a bridge there and why build it then? After all, it would be another hundred years before a second bridge was built downstream near the town. Just as Church Street Bridge was an improvement on *Átha Cliath*, so Sidney's bridge was an upgrade on the ford. It also gave access to the suburb of Kilmainham up the hill, which yields the key to the puzzle.

In 1175, in the early days of the Norman town, the lands at Kilmainham had been granted to the Knights Hospitaller of St John of Jerusalem – a papal order originally established for the medical assistance of Christians in the Holy Land, which later developed into a military establishment. They built a hospital on the site together with alms houses.

Kilmainham's good location stood to it, for the ridge it occupied commanded the view all the way east to the walled town while remaining at once both distant and near. In a sense, the order of St John – sometimes erroneously confused with the Knights Templar, a separate and often rival papal military order – had an effect on the district not unlike that of the original Celtic monastery all those centuries earlier. By having a military order astride the western approaches and defences of the capital, it commanded the most likely possible rebel routes from the interior midlands. It has served a similar military purpose in later centuries. A suburb began to form. The area became noted for its mills. The Camac, a fast-flowing tributary of the Liffey, ran downhill nearby on its way to join the larger river and facilitated this particular commercial development.

The medieval world came to a sudden end in the 1530s, with England's break with the Church of Rome, the beginnings of the Reformation and the development that bore most directly on the fortunes of Kilmainham: the dissolution of the monasteries. Just as the Vikings had put an end to the Celtic monastery, Henry VIII put an end to the Knights Hospitaller of St John of Jerusalem. The estates at Kilmainham were expropriated by the crown, thus ending almost four hundred years of history.

The monastery and lands were suppressed in 1542. There was an attempted revival under the brief reign of the Catholic Queen Mary (1553–8) but she was followed by her half-sister, the Protestant Elizabeth, who was to reign for forty-five years. That settled it. The lands at Kilmainham were vested in the crown.

Prior to the Tudor revolution, Ireland had effectively been governed in the king's name by Hiberno-Norman aristocrats. These were local warlords, usually of the House of Kildare; they were descendants of the original Normans who settled in Ireland in the late twelfth century and became a distinctive but intrinsic part of the Irish mix. Ireland was awkwardly distant from England – and especially from the seat of power in the south-east around London – so it made sense, including financial sense, to devolve Irish administration to trusted strongmen.

That arrangement had broken down irretrievably with the doomed rebellion of Silken Thomas – the last of the great magnate earls of Kildare – in 1534. Thereafter, the English crown had to take a more direct hand in the governance of Irish affairs. A succession of chief governors and senior officials came to Ireland to administer the country – or as much of it as lay within the king's writ, which was not nearly as much as they would have wished – by what we would now call direct rule.

What had been the monastery's priory house was turned into a suite of summer residences for the chief governor and his senior officials. It is worth remembering just how extensive the entire place was. It included not just the modern buildings of Kilmainham Gaol and courthouse but all the land later enclosed by the walls of the Royal Hospital. So the English officials had plenty of room for their summer holiday accommodation.

Sidney's bridge was most likely built to give them better access to this summer palace. Over time, Kilmainham developed its own particular characteristics. The extensive priory lands were effectively divided in two: the larger eastern part became the Royal Hospital and grounds, while the western part was first a place of execution – thus known as Gallows Hill – and later the site of Kilmainham Gaol. This division was cemented by the construction of the South Circular Road. Running for most of its extent east to west along the line of the Grand Canal, it was a labour of years that began in 1763. At the western margins of the city, it suddenly turned north at right angles, away from the canal, to run down the hill – making permanent the division between the Royal Hospital and Gallows Hill – to end at Islandbridge.

It rendered the bridge a kind of dead end, because immediately to the north of it was the boundary wall of the Phoenix Park. This immense green lung had been granted to the city by the Duke of Ormond in the 1660s – Ormond was viceroy of Ireland during the reign of Charles II. Moreover, it was a dead end at the wrong end of town, because it was precisely during Ormond's viceroyalty that Dublin's relentless process of northing and easting began,

Engraving of Sarah Bridge from *Dublin delineated in twenty-six views, etc* (1837)

and once started there was no stopping it. So, even to this day, the T-junction that the bridge makes with Conyngham Road – running west towards the quaint village suburb of Chapelizod and thereafter further west again clean out of town – has a somewhat apologetic, forlorn look to it.

Sidney's bridge was destroyed in a flood in 1787. It was rebuilt in 1793 and it is this structure that is still there now. It was named Sarah Bridge for Sarah Fane, Countess of Westmorland – the wife of the viceroy of the time – who laid the foundation stone in 1791.

As you cross it from south to north – that is, coming down the hill from Kilmainham – you reach the aforementioned T-junction with Conyngham Road, one of the city's great might-have-beens. Had it not been for the boundary wall of the Phoenix Park, now facing you head on, it would have made best sense to continue the circular road northward in a curving line through the park. In a mile or so, this would bring it to the park gate at the western end of the North Circular Road. Thus the two circular roads – actually long ellipses – would have been joined, creating a single orbital route around the city's margins.

But this was not done. It wasn't that there was a prohibition on running public roads through the park: there are plenty of them. The main road – Chesterfield Avenue – is one of the best in the city. Nor was there any hesitation about building in the park, although this was done judiciously: there is no concentrated building development anywhere within the park walls. Even a building as large as Áras an Uachtaráin – the residence of the president of Ireland and formerly the Viceregal Lodge – is barely noticeable in the vast green open space.

But it seems that no one ever seriously contemplated continuing the circular road through the park. There is an anomaly here, for there is a gate into the park, knocked through the wall, about a hundred yards west of the bridge – the Islandbridge Gate – which gives access to a small twisting road. So there was no taboo about gates into the park as such: there are eight in all. It's just that this more obvious means of creating a single, joined-up orbital route was not, for whatever reason, contemplated.

This raises the question of what the best alternative might be. It also introduces the fascinating figure of William Burton Conyngham (1733–96). He was an antiquarian of some distinction and a relative of Earl Conyngham of Slane Castle in County Meath. When the old earl died childless in 1781, plain William Burton – as he was up to this moment – inherited a life interest in Slane Castle and promptly settled there, tacking the extra cognomen 'Conyngham' on to his name, by which he was ever after known – largely at his own insistence. It was he who engaged James Wyatt, one of England's leading architects *du jour*, to restore the castle in the fashionable faux Gothick style, leaving it looking much as it does today.

Conyngham was also a member of the Dublin Wide Streets Commission, the most enlightened planning body the city has ever known – albeit, the competition is not strong. On the commission, Conyngham, a peppery man and an opponent of the greatest Dublin architect of the age, James Gandon, was a strong advocate for improving the road at the western approach to the north Liffey quays. This was done – he even put his own money into developing a part of it – and the result was the splendidly wide and straight Conyngham Road, quite rightly named for him. This extended east from Islandbridge as far as Parkgate – the main gate into the Phoenix Park – and thus to the bottom of what much later became Infirmary Road.

Conyngham's aim was to improve the western approaches to the city for military reasons: he was a former army officer, among other things. He wasn't worried about traffic or circular roads, but his opening of this fine road in from Islandbridge brought it within a few hundred yards of the North Circular Gate of the Phoenix Park, up the hill at the western end of Oxmantown Green. When Infirmary Road was punched through here in the 1880s, together with Conyngham Road it created the link between the two circular roads – not ideal, but a great improvement on what had previously prevailed and a fine example of the law of unintended consequences.

Until the 1970s, Islandbridge itself had a sort of edge-of-the-city feel to it. Beyond it, to the west, there were modest suburban developments but mostly centred on outlying villages – Chapelizod, Castleknock, Blanchardstown, Lucan – each of which still had that feeling of separateness that marks a village:

a kind of urban self-possession in micro. That's long gone. The west of the city is now a sprawl of shopping centres, tight-packed housing estates and exurbs touching the countryside. There are few exceptions to this asphyxiating process, but one is a little *rus in urbe* treasure: the low road to Lucan, starting at the Knockmaroon Gate of the Phoenix Park and running first downhill to the Angler's Rest pub and from there flat along that part of the river valley known as the Strawberry Beds. There are two further pubs along the few miles west to Lucan – the Strawberry Hall and the Wren's Nest – before the sprawl closes in again. Along the way, you pass under the quite spectacular span of the bridge – far above you in the sky – that carries the orbital M50 motorway across the Liffey valley. It's like something from the Italian Alps.

The sprawl is a function of wealth and easy credit. Despite the customary ups and downs, the overall performance of the Irish economy since the mid 1960s has been hugely positive. GNP per capita *trebled* in the thirty years after Ireland joined the EU in 1973. The population grew by more than 30 per cent, from three million to four million. Most of that growth was in Dublin; it is only from this time that the phrase 'Greater Dublin Area' becomes a journalistic commonplace. But the average price of a new house in Ireland grew by a factor of *twenty-five times*, far beyond anything that inflation could explain. That factor was, if anything, higher in Dublin.[1]

Thus the great *drang nach westen*. There was nowhere else to go to build all the new houses needed: the historic process of northing and easting had seen to that, having long since filled up most of the available space between the old medieval core and the bay. The arrival of the suburban railway from the 1830s had accelerated that process, especially on the south side where it hugged the coast. On the north side, the airport was in the way. To the south, the mountains were in the way. To the east, all was the briny deep. The only way was west.

Ever since the 1670s, when the northing and easting began, Islandbridge – along with the western margins in general – had fallen out of fashionable favour. It was therefore ironic that the first great monumental building in the modern city was built near here, just up the hill at the eastern end of what had been the old pre-Reformation priory lands at Kilmainham: the Royal Hospital (1684). But that was about that until the twentieth century. The city moved the other way. Then, in the dying days of British rule in Ireland, the great English architect Sir Edwin Lutyens was commissioned to design a memorial garden to the Irishmen who had died in World War I. The site chosen was at Islandbridge, on a sixty-acre site just south of the river. Although the British left in 1922, the new governments of independent Ireland – to their considerable credit, considering that attitudes to Irish participation in the war now ranged from ambiguous to outright hostile – saw this splendid memorial to completion. It opened in 1939. Shamefully, it was then left neglected and trashed for decades until restored to its original state in 1988. It is a thing of beauty.

Otherwise, the story of the western suburbs in modern times is less exhilarating. Yet that requires some qualification. Immediately to the west and south of Islandbridge, the Irish state built a series of public housing estates that provided decent, if modest, accommodation for working-class people previously trapped in the insanitary grip of the stinking downtown tenements and the vampirical landlords who had profited for too long from their misery: Ballyfermot, Drimnagh, Crumlin. A similar process took place on the other side of the Phoenix Park, in Cabra and Finglas on the north side. This was a heroic undertaking, not least because the state barely had an arse in its economic trousers when it embarked on the expenditure required.

It had, however, the unintended consequence of re-emphasising the west of the city as the locus of the less materially advantaged: in general, the western suburbs, whether entailing publicly or privately owned housing, are generally poorer than the east. A vertical line drawn north–south through Christ Church Cathedral from one city margin to the other makes this sociological reality plain.

So Islandbridge, for so long marking the city limit as surely as its river marked the tidal limit, has in a sense resumed that liminal status. It stands now at the point where urbanity yields to *les banlieues*. To the east, back towards the city centre, the mood is ever more urban, with that density of people and building stock that characterises the urban space. To the west and south, it is mostly a different kind of density that prevails: that of the spread-eagling suburbs running away towards the open country.

There is one notable exception to that generalisation. Immediately to the west of Islandbridge, at the western extension of Conyngham Road, lies the long-established urban village of Chapelizod: the chapel of Isolde. It has retained its sense of quaint unreality, a charm that is palpable but difficult to register. It is, therefore, the perfect location for the most unreal work in all of English-language fiction. James Joyce's *Finnegans Wake* – don't you fucking well dare intrude an unwanted apostrophe in there – is set in the Mullingar House pub in the village. It seems a good point at which to turn our backs on the western margins and head back into town – facing east.

– 🏵 –

THREE

RORY O'MORE BRIDGE

THE HABIT OF renaming so many bridges after heroes from the patriotic pantheon can get a little trying. This bridge is a case in point. At different times in its history, since the first version of it was built in the early 1670s, it has been known successively as Bloody Bridge, Barrack Bridge and St James's Bridge. O'More superseded them all in 1922, in the gust of earnest patriotism that heralded the birth of the Irish Free State.

The eponymous O'More was Rory of that clan, a significant political figure in the first half of the seventeenth century. The O'Mores had been long settled in possession of their ancestral lands in the midlands – modern counties Laois and Offaly – until the 1550s. Then, an early experiment in English plantation during the reign of Queen Mary (1553–8) saw them dispossessed, to be replaced by loyal and reliable English planters.

Unsurprisingly, this turned the O'Mores into rebellious malcontents. The Rory O'More for whom the bridge was renamed was a grandson of the original chieftain dispossessed. He was a consequential figure in the wars of the 1640s. By then, English rule in Ireland was fatally mixed up with the early religious Reformation, so that the rising that erupted in 1641 and lasted in one form or another until Cromwell arrived in 1649 assumed a distinctly sectarian hue. O'More himself proclaimed the union of faith and fatherland, urging unity between Gaelic and Old English families on the basis of their shared Catholicism. (The Old English were the descendants of twelfth-century Normans, long established in Ireland; like the Gaels, they had rejected the Reformation. Thus these two ethnic groups, Gaels and Old English, who had coexisted for centuries despite inevitable tensions, now began to form a common front based on confessional solidarity.)

It ended badly for Rory O'More, as with most of the rebels of the 1640s. Cromwell smashed them and finally established firm English rule in the entire island. O'More retreated westward to Inishbofin, an island in Galway Bay that was the last rebel redoubt. Failing to escape by sea, he ended up a fugitive in Ulster, where he died in the mid 1650s. None the less, his exploits were sufficient to settle him in the later nationalist succession of patriotic icons – thus the renaming of the bridge for him in 1922.

However, as with so many other well-meant name changes around this time, it didn't stick with the public. Most Dubliners couldn't tell you where O'More Bridge was, but some might be able to tell you where Watling Street Bridge is. This commonplace name marks the rather nondescript street that runs down the hill from St James's Gate on the south side to meet the river at this point. On the north side, it meets Ellis Street, insignificant now but historically much more important, for it gave access to what was then the western end of Oxmantown Green. Once more, a bridge facilitated the development and expansion of a northern suburb.

As to why it was named for Rory O'More, legend had it that during the tumult of the 1640s he made his escape across the river at this point while being pursued by crown troops.

Ellis Street, on the north side, was named for Sir William Ellis, an Englishman on the make to whom a development lease was granted, probably in 1682. He had been born around 1648, the son of a supporter of the parliamentary cause in the English civil war. He was educated at Westminster School and Christ Church Oxford, where he graduated BA in 1669. By then, with the demise of Cromwell and the restoration of Charles II in 1660, his father's parliamentary allegiance was a distant memory and a lost cause. The younger Ellis accommodated himself effortlessly to the restored monarchy and established himself in Ireland. There was no shortage of enterprising rascals profiting personally from the final English conquest of Ireland – effected with exemplary brutality by Cromwell in the 1640s – and Ellis was conspicuous among them.

He acquired various sinecures of profit in the 1670s and even rose to be chief secretary from 1682 to 1685. By the former year, he had clearly acquired a sufficient fortune to pay for the grant of land along the western margin of the north bank of the Liffey. The viceroy, Ormond, disliked him and accused him of avarice. But Ormond's fortunes dipped with the death of his patron Charles II in 1685, whereupon Ellis – a veritable Vicar of Bray – transferred his allegiance to the Duke of Tyrconnell, the favourite of the new king, James II. James was the last Catholic king of England, and Tyrconnell pursued an aggressive policy of re-Catholicising the Irish royal administration, including – to the alarm of the newly established post-Cromwellian Protestant landed class – the military. Ellis, although a Protestant, was active in these endeavours, and when it all ended badly for James and Tyrconnell he followed them into exile in France. He died in Rome.

The purpose of Ellis's grant was to help develop the lands of Oxmantown westward in the direction of what is now the Phoenix Park, spreading out from its core around St Michan's and Church Street. The bridge built here as part of his development was almost certainly not the first bridge on the site. While we have no knowledge of earlier structures, it seems certain by inference that there must have been some sort of crossing here to connect to the fledgling north-side development that was later formalised by Ellis's grant.

According to architectural historian Maurice Craig, this grant entailed all the land from Church Street Bridge to what is now the Parkgate, which is the main entrance to the Phoenix Park and the one nearest to the river and the developing city.[1] Parkgate is about halfway between Church Street Bridge and Islandbridge. J.T. Gilbert (1829–98), the first great scholarly historian of the city, notes that Ellis's grant did not come cheap. He records how Ellis 'laid out considerable sums of money in purchasing ground in Oxmantowne [sic], with design to make a quay along the river to the Parke [sic] wall, and to make a considerable addition of buildings there, to the honour, beauty and profit of the city'. As we shall see in chapter 6, Ellis was also responsible for the first crossing at what is now Mellowes Bridge, just upriver of Church Street Bridge, joining what is now Queen Street on the north side to Bridgefoot Street on the south, leading up to St Catherine's Church on Thomas Street.

That lay sometime in the future when Ellis was planning his first bridge, around 1682, upon his purchase of the development lease from the city fathers. His first structure here was wooden, echoing that which we infer must have been in place already. Indeed, historian Douglas Bennett states that this previous wooden bridge had been erected in 1674 and was known as Barrack Bridge.[2] This name would have been anachronistic in the 1670s because the barracks referred to could only have been the Royal Barracks, not built until 1701. It is now Collins Barracks and home to the second campus of the National Museum of Ireland. At any rate, this earlier bridge was sufficiently real to have prompted a fatal affray, as follows.

There was a ferry service on the river at this point, and obviously any bridge at all was going to be hostile to the commercial interests of the ferrymen. The upshot was a riot in support of the ferrymen. They had encouraged a mob to protest against the bridge, which protest turned ugly and prompted the city authorities to haul about twenty of the protesters off to the Bridewell. An attempt to rescue these lads from the clutches of the authorities resulted in the deaths of four of the protesters.

So this earlier structure may have been elusive in terms of solid, verifiable written records (Bennett, a careful, scholarly man, did not cite a source for his assertion but hardly invented it). One way or another, this earlier wooden bridge was sufficiently substantial that lads thought it worth their lives. Clearly there was something there worth fighting over. It is reasonable, on the basis of probability, to accept that whatever structure was there in 1674 was something real and not a phantom, thus making it a few years older than Grattan Bridge, downriver at Capel Street, which would otherwise have claimed the prize of being the second-oldest bridge over the urban Liffey and which – as we shall soon see – was a crossing of vastly greater significance for the city's subsequent development than Ellis's effort.

The fatal affray also accounted for one of the many names the bridge bore: Bloody Bridge. It held that name in popular usage for a long time, despite changing formal names. In *Ulysses*, Joyce – who was scrupulous about getting details like this right – refers to it thus in a passage describing the procession of the viceroy's party making its way from the Viceregal Lodge in the Phoenix Park to a social function. He notes that as the viceroy took the loyal salutes of various pedestrians, 'at Bloody Bridge Mr Thomas Kernan beyond the river greeted him vainly from afar'.

By the early 1680s, therefore, Ellis's bridge – whether named Bloody Bridge or Barrack Bridge – was up. The wooden structure was replaced by a stone bridge in the first decade of the eighteenth century, just as the Royal Barracks was being built nearby; it was officially called Barrack Bridge thereafter. However, if there is one thing more than another that can be confusing about these

Barrack Bridge, c. 1813–37, with Queen's (Mellowes) Bridge in the background

Liffey bridges, it is the successive profusion of changing official and popular names. This bridge was next briefly named St James's Bridge and then from 1861 – to mark Her Majesty's gracious visit to the Hibernian metropolis – Victoria Bridge. Old Vic got bumped for Rory O'More, as we saw, in 1922. But what really stuck was the original moniker, Bloody Bridge, which accounts for the Joycean reference.

These days, whatever name is used, it's likely unfamiliar to most Dubliners. There is no surprise there, for this is a dead end of the city to which people pay little attention. It is a recurring theme of Dublin history: for all the fun cranked out of north-side–south-side jokes, the east–west divide has been far more consequential. And O'More Bridge occupies just about the sleepiest part of the west inner city.

The city authorities have undertaken various initiatives over the years in attempts to inject some civic energy into this quarter, the National Museum in Collins Barracks and the development of Smithfield as a civic centre being the two most notable. Yet fashion remains stubbornly east of Capel Street Bridge, although behind the museum on the north side – in Stoneybatter, Manor Street and the little streets off Oxmantown Road and Arbour Hill – a market-driven process of gentrification has generated a bourgeois-boho quarter in the last generation, as young professionals driven out of more established areas by soaring purchase prices for houses have settled there.

Still, Rory O'More Bridge is one of the Liffey crossings that defies the normal rule that holds that a bridge leads directly to urban development on either side of the river – usually the north side in the early days. But this bridge is a kind of pontine apology, going from nowhere to nowhere.

A number of city maps were published in the last third of the seventeenth century but it wasn't until Charles Brooking's map of 1728 that we can see the dramatic effect of the various bridges that were constructed after 1670. The density of development on the north side shown by Brooking is in stark contrast to the patchy settlements around Church Street and St Michan's on Speed's map. By now, in the mere course of a single century in a town about eight hundred years old, the north side has spread from east of Bloody Bridge – for, thanks to stubborn popular usage, that is how Brooking marks it – as far north as King Street and as far across as Marlborough Street, well downriver to the east. In short, the north side looks for the first time like the proper half of a city. But poor old Bloody Bridge is still adrift at its western margin, and in an odd way it has retained that liminal quality, despite dense development all around in later times.

Some of that early development is shown on what was perhaps the very finest ever map of Dublin, at least prior to the Ordnance Survey: that made by John Rocque in 1756. Significant buildings are now established in the western margins – the Royal Hospital and Dr Steevens's Hospital conspicuous among them – but otherwise the area had to await the nineteenth century for further urban expansion. The building of the Grand Canal and its basin; the growing economic influence of Guinness and other breweries and distilleries; and the arrival of the railway, with the terminus of the Great Southern & Western (1844) just downriver of Bloody Bridge at Kingsbridge/Heuston all contributed to the quickening of social and economic life in the south-western quadrant. But they also further identified the area as commercial and industrial, and therefore not fashionable.

Even as early as Rocque's map, the traffic is shown to be firmly in the other direction. The process of northing and easting is now under way with a vengeance. On the north side, most of the lands south of Dorset Street as far as the river – including the early version of Sackville Street – are shown as built-up. A generation later, towards the end of the eighteenth century, the building of the new Custom House downriver of Sackville Street pushed the commercial heart of the city further eastward, while on the south side developments were dramatic. Less than thirty years before Rocque, Brooking had shown the embryonic Stephen's Green at the south-eastern margins of the city. Now, in the 1750s, it is shown fully laid out and developed and an integral part of the urban fabric. Moreover, Merrion Square, just around the corner, will begin its development a few years later.

So, on both sides of the river the beating pulse of the city was moving ever farther from Bloody Bridge. It remained what it had been from the beginning: a plain, basic structure. Moreover, as time passed it became a less stable one, an alarming fault in a bridge. In 1805, the city grand jury adverted to its dangerous condition. The response was something of a depressing pattern where Dublin bridges were concerned: dither and delay rather than prompt action. We saw in chapter 1 that it took almost two hundred years to sort out similar problems of decay and neglect at Church Street Bridge. So, typically, for almost fifty years after the grand-jury alarm call, nothing happened other than minimal patch-ups.

Then there came to the rescue a father and son who might be the heroes of any Dublin story. For the first half of the nineteenth century George Halpin (c. 1774–1854) was the inspector of works – in effect, principal engineer – to the Ballast Board, the statutory authority in charge of the port of Dublin. Among other things,

Legend has it that Rory O'More made his escape from crown troops at this point across the Liffey in 1641

this remarkably gifted man built lighthouses all around the Irish coast, including the Baily Lighthouse on Howth Head. He was also closely involved in the construction of the Bull Wall at Clontarf, which, projecting into the harbour, created a pinch point with the Poolbeg Lighthouse opposite at the end of the Great South Wall. (He also superintended improvements to the Poolbeg Lighthouse.) The effect of the pinch point at the entrance to the Liffey estuary was that the ebb tide scoured away the sand and silt that had been a navigational curse on the river for centuries. It facilitated the subsequent development of the modern port.

Halpin was one of those who heeded the successive warnings about Bloody Bridge and suggested improvements and other patch-ups; but most of all, he recommended that an entirely new bridge be built. He did not live to see this done but his son – also George Halpin – who had succeeded him in office did. After further delays and disputes, a design by Halpin junior for a single-span metal design was accepted and the necessary contracts with providers and suppliers entered into. Thus was built the structure that we see today. It was begun in 1858 and completed by late 1861, by which time the principal contractor had gone bust.

It was named for Queen Victoria on her penultimate visit to Ireland in 1861. She actually crossed the bridge just before it was finally finished. She did not, however, formally open it; that was done the following year.

It is not a thing of beauty, being plain and minimally adorned. But it is tactful. It knows its place – modest, discreet and unostentatious – which is appropriate to this relatively narrow part of the river and to a corner of the city that has resisted the introduction of urban bustle. In this, it stands in dignified contrast to the next bridge downstream, the ludicrously disproportionate Calatrava-designed James Joyce Bridge, which might be a splendid piece of design but is in the wrong place. We shall meet it properly later.

— ❦ —

FOUR

GRATTAN BRIDGE

N OW WE'RE TRAVELLING. This is arguably the most important bridge ever thrown across the Liffey. It is east, if only just, of the medieval town around Christ Church. The river ran free at the quays below, unhindered by any crossing until Church Street/Fr Mathew Bridge, a little to the west, effectively marked the commercial edge of the little town.

Dublin's entire urban life had to do with trade, goods inwards and outwards, and for centuries most of this business was discharged on the quays below Christ Church, what today are – working upriver from east to west – Wellington Quay, Wood Quay and Merchants Quay. It was obvious that any bridge constructed along these quays would have the effect of pushing the commercial boundary of the river downstream to the east, as it would hinder – if not totally block – the further passage of shipping upstream.

So centuries of tradition, with the associated established commercial vested interests, were invested in this stretch of urban fabric. Customs duties were discharged in a premises, now lost to history, at a site on Wellington Quay. It was clearly a substantial premises to judge from surviving accounts. It was built throughout the seventeenth century and by the end of the century served more ceremonial state functions than mere customs clearance – although obviously it still did that as its basic duty – such as the swearing in of newly arrived viceroys in its council chamber. This chamber, which appears to have been an impressive room, was also the site of Privy Council meetings. Other rooms in the complex were used from time to time for parliamentary committee meetings, especially in the period following the Stuart restoration when the Irish parliament ceased to be peripatetic and settled in a permanent residence at Chichester House in College Green, later rebuilt as the magnificent parliament house and now sadly come down in the world as the prize and unworthy possession of the Bank of Ireland.

Bridging the river at or near this point would have the inevitable effect of restricting shipping to the east, thus nudging the commercial limit of the city a little in that direction – away from what is now Wood Quay and Merchants Quay – and settling it decisively on Wellington Quay. As if to copper-fasten this process, a wholly new Custom House was built on Wellington Quay in 1707. Designed by Thomas Burgh, who was also responsible for the Royal Barracks mentioned in the last chapter and for the magnificent Old Library in Trinity College, it proved the least successful of his works and, unlike the other structures just mentioned, it did not long survive. Although it appears an imposing building, judging from old prints, it quickly became clear that it was too small and of unsuitable design for its primary purpose. As early as 1770, only about one ship in eight trading on the Liffey loaded or discharged goods at this quay, finding it more convenient to do so farther downriver in deeper water. As

View of the Custom House from Samuel Frederick Brocas's 'Select Views of Dublin'

Dublin's commercial life grew and grew, it pushed everything downriver to the east, leading to the eventual abandonment of this old Custom House and the building of a new one – James Gandon's masterpiece – in its current location below Butt Bridge.

Capel St/Grattan Bridge was integral to this drawn-out historical process. It was completed in 1678, long before Burgh's custom house was built but part of the same impulse. Its construction was naturally and understandably opposed by the merchants of the old town, long accustomed to the unimpeded flow of commercial shipping craft as far upriver as Church Street/ Fr Mathew Bridge – which had, after all, been there more or less for ever. They feared that any such bridge could only help to open up another segment of the north bank to their collective disadvantage, established as they were on the other shore. In this apprehension, they were proved to be absolutely justified, for no single structure in the history of Dublin has had a greater or more permanent effect on the development of the north side than this bridge.

Its prime mover was Sir Humphrey Jervis, whose memory survives in a street name, a shopping centre, a tram stop and a former city hospital. He was another Englishman settled in Ireland in pursuit of his fortune, rather like Sir William Ellis of Bloody Bridge. Born in 1630 to a family with roots in Shropshire and Staffordshire, he was not only in Dublin by the time he was about twenty-five, he was – even at that young age – a freeman of the city. Later, he became an alderman and city sheriff. These were significant offices indicative of wealth and rank: an alderman, for instance, could be a senior member of a guild, or a magistrate, or representing an area of the city at a rank only below that of mayor. In fact, Jervis himself was lord mayor in 1681 and 1682, thus ascending to the top of the municipal tree. He was wealthy and played a significant role in the commercial life of the growing town. Indeed, it might be said that he was one of those whose efforts helped to propel Dublin from town status to that of a city.

Like every good developer before and since, he knew that there were opportunities for making money on vacant sites on the edge of town. In the 1670s, the undeveloped edge of town was north of the river. Up to that point, the north side – as exiguous as suggested by the scattered buildings shown on Speed's map (1610) – had been robbed of one of its few built complexes of substance. This was St Mary's Abbey, lying ruinous since the dissolution of the monasteries in the previous century. It had been established in 1139 and within a decade of its foundation had passed into the possession and keeping of the Cistercians. This order, a key modernising force in medieval Ireland, was established on the island even before the arrival of the Normans. Along with Mellifont to the north of Dublin, St Mary's was one of the order's key foundations. Moreover, it was the biggest single complex – in terms of area – north of the river. It occupied a site approximating to the modern block of streets just west of Capel Street.

But after the depredations of Henry VIII in the late 1530s, it was wrecked like so many similar foundations across the British Isles. Its stones lay scattered until Sir Humphrey Jervis saw a use for them more than a century later. Jervis had the ear of the viceroy, Arthur Capel, earl of Essex. Into the viceroy's ear he poured blandishments. He would use the stones of St Mary's Abbey to construct a new bridge that would open up the north side of the river, where he proposed to develop further. Its principal street, running north from the river to link with the western end of Drumcondra Lane, the main route out of the town to the north (now Dorset Street), would be called Capel Street and the bridge to gain access to it would be named Essex Bridge. All of this happened, with the bridge retaining the Essex name until 1875 when it was renamed for Henry Grattan, the eighteenth-century colonial patriot.

All this was done in the face of outright hostility from the existing city merchant elite. Their material interests all lay south of the river, in the historic centre, and they were reflexively hostile to this démarche to the north side. Their anxieties were justified when Jervis had the city markets moved from the old town to his new north-side domain during his term as lord mayor, on the ancient principle that what's the use of power if you can't abuse it. Not only that, the south-side merchants accused Jervis of various other kinds of crooked dealing. As you might expect, they were hardly disinterested spectators of Jervis's operations, but it is unlikely that their accusations were entirely ill-founded. Sir Humphrey was, after all, an 'improver' or what we would now refer to as a property developer. It was not a vocation, then or since, for the fastidious or the over-scrupulous, so we may reasonably infer that Jervis was not behind the door when it came to cutting corners.

Yet for all that, he was the sort of person who got things done. It was as a result of his energy and enterprise that the bridge was built, that Capel Street was laid out and that it represented the open sesame to the further and dense development of the north side. Moreover, he did it for the greater part with his own money, for his initial patron, Essex, was recalled to England in 1677 and replaced by the restored Ormond. This man, one of the great figures of Irish history about whom we know a fair amount but not nearly half enough – will anyone out there please write a thorough full-length scholarly biography of the man and his times? – stepped in as Essex's replacement patron. But, crucially, he claimed not to have the funds to support Jervis's ambition, leaving Sir Humphrey to risk his own capital, which he did – rather heroically, if not actually recklessly – in a manner that, like many developers before and since, resulted in his acute financial embarrassment.

But still: the viceroy had made one crucial suggestion, or perhaps it was a stipulation, that was decisive for the future and further development of Dublin. He instructed Jervis to extend the existing embankment of the Liffey alongside his new north-side holdings – thus the creation of Ormond Quay – and to have the newly developed properties on the riverbank constructed face on to the river, with a carriageway for traffic between it and the houses. Thus Dublin turned its face to the river where previously it had been inclined to show its arse.

Jervis's five-hundred-year north-side lease, granted sometime around 1676, cost him £3,000 up front, so it was hardly surprising that he later found himself strapped when his successive viceregal patrons, Essex and Ormond, declined, refused or were genuinely unable to chip in, leaving Sir Humphrey to shoulder the financial burden alone. It did not stop his rise to the mayoralty, but that was the summit of his achievement. Once again, events beyond his control conspired against him and gave his enemies on the city council – mostly representatives of material and commercial interests hostile to his ambitions – their opportunity.

In 1685, the king, Charles II, died without legitimate issue to be replaced by his brother James, a Catholic. Ormond, Charles's strong right arm in Ireland for the best part of twenty-five years, was recalled. James inserted new men, most of them of a hyper-Catholic disposition, into the Irish administration. Jervis found few friends or protectors there, which opened the door for those in the city council who had hated him for years to seize their opportunity. They pressed such charges against him that they secured his imprisonment for ten months over the winter of 1685–6.

None the less, Jervis's legacy is secure. He, more than anyone else, oversaw early dense development on his north-side holdings and in doing so effectively urbanised that side of the river. It was a process of generations but his was the vital motor that started it. Perhaps someone else would have done it; perhaps it looks in retrospect so obvious that if it hadn't been Sir Humphrey it would, of necessity, have been someone else unknown. But there's the rub: unknown. We only know what actually happened, and what actually happened was that Sir Humphrey Jervis was the one whose exertions first opened up the north side of the Liffey to housing and commerce – no one else.

In so doing, he built the bridge that still marks the east–west divide in Dublin and laid out Capel Street as the main drag in his new domain. Most of the future development of the city was to take place east of Capel St/Essex/Grattan Bridge. This process did not just create a new urban quarter on the previously neglected side of the river; rather this process turned Dublin from a town to a city. The growth of Dublin in the hundred years after Jervis was phenomenal, so that by the middle years of the eighteenth century it was already being spoken of as one of the most substantial cities in Europe.

The principal streets developed off Capel Street were Mary Street and Great Britain Street, both running east, eventually to link up with the area around what is now O'Connell Street; this area was first developed by Henry Moore, earl of Drogheda, and later by the Gardiner estate. In the case of the earl, he left us with his names: thus Henry Street, Moore Street, Earl Street and Drogheda Lane, the original name of what later became Sackville

A view of Essex Bridge, c. 1790

Street and later again O'Connell Street. There was even an Of
Lane, shown on Rocque's map as Off Lane and now called Henry
Place, just off Henry Street. So old Henry the earl had done
himself proud and awarded himself a full house. We shall meet
him again, and the Gardiners, later in this book. Great Britain
Street, incidentally, got its patriotic name change in 1911: we
know it as Parnell Street.

Mary Street was the first of these side streets to be developed. It
was named for St Mary's Church, designed by William Robinson,
also responsible for the Royal Hospital (1684) in the relatively
remote south-western quadrant of the city but which was none
the less the first great civic structure built in the city after the
Restoration. St Mary's is dated to 1697 and even at this date is
establishing the city's future direction of travel: to the east. Douglas
Bennett describes it as 'the most important classical church to
survive the 17th century'.[1] In its turn, the church had been named
for St Mary's Abbey, which had stood nearby and whose stones,
as we have seen, had been used by Jervis to build Essex Bridge.
It was in St Mary's that Theobald Wolfe Tone, born around the
corner at 44 Stafford Street (the street that now bears his name),
was baptised. It remained in the care of the Church of Ireland until
parish numbers had so fallen away by the 1970s that the church sold
it. For a time, it was used as a place of worship by the city's Greek
Orthodox community until it was completely secularised and sold
to a developer in 1988. It is now a pub/restaurant styling itself The
Church Café, which sounds ghastly but isn't: many features of the
original church have been sensitively retained.

As Maurice Craig remarks of Jervis's new bridge: 'Essex Bridge
itself became immediately the focal point of Dublin, remaining
so for more than a hundred years.'[2] Indeed it did, until the rise

of Drogheda Lane/Sackville/O'Connell Street to become the
city's principal, and only, boulevard, although you'd hardly call
it a boulevard now, so tawdry has it become in modern times,
despite some sterling efforts at renewal that are impressive in
themselves – I *love* the Spire – but don't aggregate to anything
architecturally coherent. Fashion has long since abandoned the
north side for the south. O'Connell Street, as the main north-
side street, has declined accordingly. That's before you factor in
nineteenth-century vandalism and neglect, not to mention the
catastrophic destruction of its urban fabric by the Easter Rising
of 1916 and the Civil War of 1922–3.

In the century after the erection of Grattan Bridge and the
opening to the north side, Capel Street became the hinge on
which the process of northing and easting swung. By the time of
John Rocque's map (1756) the undertaking is well in hand. To
the north, it shows the development of Bolton Street and Upper
Dorset Street as far as Dominick Street, and from the southern end
of Dominick Street further east – past the beginnings of Sackville
Street Upper – to Marlborough Street, thus consolidating the
process begun earlier eastward from Bloody Bridge.

The really spectacular further development of the north side
pushing east is shown with startling clarity on the Ordnance
Survey Six-Inch Map of 1837: it is barely 150 years after the
first opening of Capel Street by Sir Humphrey Jervis, this in a
city that had hardly witnessed any significant physical growth in
the preceding three centuries. By 1837, the north side is almost
as densely developed and settled as the south side. Dorset Street
still marks the most prominent north-west boundary – although
some streets off it, such as Eccles Street, further to its west had
already been completed by 1820 – as far as the North Circular

Road and towards the Royal Canal a little further on at Binns Bridge. This latter was named for one John Binns, a mercer of colonial patriot sympathies who had been an early investor in the canal. The canal, however, did not pay its way and the investors never even recouped their capital, let alone earned dividends on it. Its difficulties were often blamed on the supersession of the canals by the railway, but in fact it was not so with either the Grand or the Royal Canals: their commercial failure antedated the arrival of the railway by decades.

The eastern boundary of the north side was now the circular road pushing south-east to meet Amiens Street and the North Strand at the Five Lamps junction. Within this new embrace lay Mountjoy Square – the nearest of all the Georgian squares to a mathematical square – and Gandon's new Custom House. Even beyond this point, the 1837 map shows the early further development to the north-east towards Ballybough and Fairview/ Clontarf. On the seaward side, this was all reclaimed land, as the name North Strand implies.

Also within this new north-side embrace, at its south-eastern margin beside the Five Lamps (a lamp standard dating from much later, in the last quarter of the nineteenth century) lies what is the last great classical private house built in Dublin, and the saddest. This is Aldborough House, dating from the fateful year of 1798, and built as the urban residence of Edward Stratford, 2nd earl of Aldborough. When new, it was on the edge of the city, a veritable *rus in urbe* with a marine view clear across to the bay uninterrupted by the as yet undeveloped North Lotts to the east of North Strand Road. These lots – there were eventually 132 of them – were subsequently developed by the lot-holders, mainly as small cottage-style dwellings running towards East Wall and the western end of Clontarf Road, although later separated from both by the embankment of the Great Northern Railway making its way out of Amiens Street Station (now Connolly) towards Belfast.

The earl did not live long to enjoy his new house. In truth, it is a rather disappointing building with a granite façade that is flat and plain, a big top-heavy lummox of a thing. But it hardly deserved its fate. A few years after the earl's death, it was sold and became a school, then – shamefully – a military barracks. Later it was used as a post-office store, both in the later days of British rule and in the early decades of independence, before being abandoned altogether in the 1970s. It has been woefully neglected, unprotected by the city authorities and prey to vandals whose depredations threatened the structural stability of the house. It became a temple to the very worst of Dublin philistinism. It still stands forlorn, a hulking presence surrounded by unsympathetic neighbouring buildings. However, there are ambitious development plans afoot to restore it, make it structurally safe and develop an office complex on its wings. As of the time of writing (early 2022) this project has not advanced, having – among other things – been subject to the drearily predictable objections of some conservation groups. The practical choice for this big, disproportionate house is development or destruction.

That's enough easting for the moment because we need to go back into town and turn, for almost the last time, to Sir Humphrey Jervis.

His enterprise, doubtless assisted by the sharp practice without which no 'improver', then or now, could long survive, had, as we saw, been crucial to the opening up and development of the north side. But these early bridges also had their effect on the south side. The most important effect of Grattan Bridge was to prompt demands for a street running straight from its southern end. This eventually became Parliament Street. There is some confusion as to when exactly the work on this street was first undertaken. Brooking's map of 1728 clearly shows a short street, rendered by him as being as wide as the bridge, running the few steps to Essex Street. Almost thirty years later, Rocque's map shows the same street. Although this is only the lesser part of what we now call Parliament Street, it is clear that the opening of the bridge facilitated early development on the southern shore.

The streets all around this area otherwise remained a medieval tangle. Then, in 1757, an act was made to extend and open up this embryonic street to link it with Dame Street and thus give a new route via Dame Street to College Green and the parliament house – ergo the name. It was one of the first city developments overseen by the newly formed Wide Streets Commission, an enlightened body of the great and the good which was to prove the finest planning authority the city has ever known – not, in fairness, a high bar to clear.

At the junction with Dame Street it was proposed to build a display square in the shadow of the castle but that plan was never realised. Instead the Royal Exchange (now City Hall) was built on the site to the design of Thomas Cooley of London, this award being much to the chagrin of the Dublin architects, not least the great James Gandon who came second – always worse than coming last.

The judges were well-justified in their choice, however, and what is now City Hall is one of the finest buildings in Dublin. It is the only major building in the city designed by Cooley, although he contributed a number of other minor ones – not all of which have survived. Its foundation stone was laid in 1769; the building opened as an exchange ten years later and continued to perform that function until it was ceded to the Dublin Corporation in 1852.

It was all a straw in the wind. Henceforth – certainly from the 1740s – the centre of fashionable development moved south of the river. The north side had had a good start and did not atrophy, but the force was with not just the other side of the river but also its south-eastern margin. St Stephen's Green was fully developed by the mid-century, and the streets between it and Trinity – Dawson Street (1710s and '20s), Molesworth Street (1740s and '50s), Grafton Street (from 1708 on) et al. – were already in place.

The reason that this area had been considered unsuitable for development was that it was low lying, swampy and prone to flooding. And the farther east you pushed from Leinster House, the worse that problem was. None the less, it was here, in Kildare Street, that the Earl of Leinster – Ireland's premier peer – decided to build his great town house. Fashion followed him, and the drainage problems were resolved, although even as late as 1792 a storm on the lower Liffey caused the retaining walls to breach on Sir John Rogerson's Quay, resulting in widespread flooding. So bad was it that a group of young bucks took a rowing boat, shot the breach in the quay wall and sailed all the way up to one of the back gardens in Merrion Square. That's about a distance of a kilometre of gently rising ground, so it held enough water for a small boat to sail it. What larks for the bucks!

—⚜—

FIVE

O'DONOVAN ROSSA BRIDGE

B ACK IN THE late seventeenth century, having superintended and financed the building of Grattan Bridge, Jervis now further honoured his patron by building a second bridge, just upstream of the first, called Ormond Bridge. That was in 1682, when Sir Humphrey was lord mayor. This new bridge was put up at the suggestion of some leading men on the city council; it was a wooden structure whose purpose was to give access to the Ormond Market, which, as we have seen, had been relocated by Jervis to his new holdings on the north bank of the river, just behind Ormond Quay. There the market remained until the late nineteenth century, when it was demolished to make way for what is now Ormond Square. As late as 1862, *Thom's Directory* lists six victuallers, an oilman (actually a woman, Mrs Hogg), a fishmonger, two poulterers (one of whom supplied the viceroy) and a fruiterer as trading from the market.

Ormond Market was not merely a placid place of commerce. In the middle years of the eighteenth century it was also home ground to the Ormond Boys, young men principally engaged in the victualling and allied trades. They were Catholics – aggressively so. No less aggressive were the Liberty Boys, mainly weavers from the Liberties and robustly Protestant; many were of Huguenot descent, part of that French Protestant diaspora that followed the 1685 Revocation of the Edict of Nantes, which had previously guaranteed religious toleration in France. On and off through the eighteenth century, these two factions engaged in running battles, each looking to 'occupy' the other's territory and inflicting horrible injuries and even deaths on captives.

Dublin had no police force in any modern sense, only a feeble parish-watch system. This was utterly ineffective in the face of rioting of such intensity, although the violence usually burned itself out after a few days. Still, for those days, the centre of Dublin – not least its bridges, which gave each faction potential access to the other's territory – was effectively a no-go area for law-abiding citizens. The riots in 1759, however, were of a different order. They spilled down Dame Street and threatened the parliament house itself. The precincts of parliament were breached and MPs and peers roughly handled. That prompted a more robust response from the authorities: cavalry were deployed to restore order; the law against riot was generally toughened up. The serenity of Georgian Dublin, represented so graphically in paintings and engravings as to constitute a later visual folk memory of time and place, was by no means the whole picture. Classical Dublin was a rough town, as we shall see again.

Ormond Market was replaced by the Wholesale Fruit and Vegetable Market built by the Dublin Corporation in 1892 in nearby Mary's Lane. This was part of an early effort at slum clearance in the city. In 1876, a Dr Mapother had identified twelve 'unhealthy areas' in need of street widening and urban renewal.

Ormond Market and its immediate environs was identified as one such. A scholarly article in an academic journal by one S. Harty in 1884 identified the prevailing conditions in such areas as 'a high incidence of zymotic diseases [ones supposedly but incorrectly spread by invisible gasses], lung disease and rheumatism, low tone of general health, filthy habits, intemperance, and debased morals'.[1]

So access to the original Ormond Market had been the ostensible reason for Jervis's second bridge. He built a simple – perhaps too simple – wooden structure. Finished in 1682, it had no railings. It only lasted a couple of years before the city authorities pulled it down and built a stone bridge either on the same site or just beside it. The name Ormond Bridge was retained. But the foundations of this bridge were set in one of the marshiest and least reliable parts of the Liffey bed and its stability was always an issue. Engineers had for years been predicting its collapse but, in the finest tradition of the Dublin city authorities, nothing more than desultory patching and mending was done, and in December 1802 the inevitable happened. During a tidal inundation that accompanied a winter storm, the bridge collapsed. It was not replaced. Instead, a new bridge was built nearby and named Richmond Bridge, to honour the Duchess of Richmond – the vicereine – who laid the foundation stone. It opened in 1816 and still stands.

This structure is, therefore, the only one of the bridges considered in this book which is addressed out of the strict sequence of its construction. But it was really a replacement/continuation of the defunct Ormond Bridge, which accounts for the anomaly. It was not built on the same site: perhaps the city fathers, having been once bitten by the unstable foundations of the earlier bridge, wanted its replacement to be more solidly grounded.

There was another consideration. Shortly before Ormond Bridge collapsed, the Four Courts building – Gandon's second riverine masterpiece – was completed, in 1802, although its construction had been sufficiently advanced by 1796 for the courts to first function there in that year. It made every sense to orient the new bridge on this monumental building, now the epicentre of the Irish legal system.

It was, in a sense, a return to base for the lawyers. As early as 1610, Speed's map shows a building marked 'The Inns' at the western end of the current site, hard by Church Street/Fr Mathew Bridge. However, this proved a temporary arrangement only, for – as with so many other things involving potential or actual north-side developments – vested interests still lay south of the river and that is where the courts were to reside for the next two hundred years or so.

The Four Courts and Richmond Bridge as depcited by William Sadler the Younger (1782–1839)

The inns of courts accordingly established themselves on the south side. At the time of Speed's map, they were in Hoggen (now College) Green, in a building originally built for wounded and infirm ex-soldiers, a sort of royal hospital *avant la lettre*, which in turn passed into the ownership of Sir Arthur Chichester, the lord deputy and one of the principal beneficiaries of the crown's successful war against Hugh O'Neill's rebellion that ended at the Battle of Kinsale (1601). Chichester, best known as the founder of Belfast, where a number of city-centre streets are still named for him, built his Dublin town house here, just down the way from the castle. The site later became that of the parliament house, now (sadly, how have the mighty fallen) a bank.

So our learned friends had to move. Their new site was in a premises in the wing of Christ Church Cathedral, already itself in a state of decay and to remain so until the beneficence of Henry Roe the distiller restored it and augmented it to its current condition in the second half of the nineteenth century. From the very start, the building was something of a wreck and unsuitable for its purpose. The lawyers were established on this site by the early sixteenth century and despite the building's shortcomings – its approach from the east was along a partially arched walkway known simply as 'Hell' – were, in the characteristic manner of the Dublin elite through the centuries, resistant to change and reluctant to move.

But the pressure to do so grew and in time became irresistible. The actual process that delivered the inns of court back to the banks of the Liffey involved some horse trading. A tussle had been going on since the 1770s concerning the old Custom House at what is now Wellington Quay. It was cramped and unfit for purpose; John Beresford, the younger son of the earl of Tyrone, was the most forceful and influential man in the Irish administration, and he wanted to relocate the Custom House farther downriver to the east. This met with the inevitable resistance from those interests who were apprehensive about any significant development away from the city core. But Beresford eventually got his way, only to be stymied by London.

This impediment was caused by one Wellbore Ellis, a member of Lord North's cabinet. He was a descendant of William Ellis, of Bloody Bridge fame, and he had inherited the Ellis estate which, as we saw earlier, ran along the north bank of the river and included, at its eastern end, the site of the current Four Courts. Ellis shared the fears of those who predicted that moving the Custom House downriver would impact negatively on remaining properties upriver. So he wanted a deal: in return for agreeing to the proposed new Custom House site, he wanted a major public development on his land. At the time, it was intended to move the courts from their hopeless location at Christ Church down Dame Street towards College Green. That plan was binned in order to overcome Ellis's objection and a new site on his holdings – the present one – was agreed.

There was already a small development on the site. At its western end, Thomas Cooley had designed a building to house state records. However, the commission for the new courts building – which would include and subsume Cooley's building – went instead to James Gandon, a pupil of Sir William Chambers, who had been beaten by Cooley in the competition for the Royal Exchange. Gandon duly removed from London to Dublin in 1781.

He quickly established a rapport with Beresford, who was a good man to know, but not with everyone else of influence among the city authorities. Principal among Gandon's adversaries was William Burton Conyngham, whom we have met already in the chapter on Islandbridge, he who was responsible for Conyngham Road. He was an assertive member of the Wide Streets Commissioners and a persistent thorn in Gandon's flesh. But his objections, and those of others who resented Gandon's closeness to Beresford, were eventually overborne and the new courts building, with its huge drum roof and internal rotunda, soon came to dominate the upper reaches of the urban Liffey, as it does to this day.

So it made a certain sense to locate a bridge with such ready access to it. However, unlike the other bridges originally built in the last quarter of the seventeenth century – as with the defunct Ormond Bridge – it contributed next to nothing to the development of the north side. That process carried on merrily without it, running – as we have seen – east from Bloody Bridge up to the line of Dorset Street and the North Circular Road. Richmond Bridge, as it then was, may have given access to the Four Courts, but once on the north side it declined into a side street, now Chancery Place, then making a dog leg that becomes first Greek Street and then Beresford Street and finally petering out where it meets North King Street, which ran west to east along the northern margin of the expanding city towards Dorset Street. It was neither one thing nor the other: Church Street was on one side of it, Capel Street on the other, and the space between mostly taken up with Ormond Market. It is still a nondescript area.

The south side of the bridge was a different matter. It gives onto Winetavern Street, one of the oldest streets in the city. It appears to have been laid out at least as early as the late eleventh century – that is in Viking times, before the arrival of the Normans. In its early years, the street possessed a great many grog shops and other places where alcohol was dispensed, ergo the name.

Winetavern Street roughly corresponds to the westerly line of the Viking walled town, just as Exchange Street roughly marks the line of the eastern wall. To the south the wall ran west to east following the line of the Poddle as it made its way towards the Liffey, wrapping round – as it bends north for the last few hundred metres – the fortified site that later, under the Normans, grew into Dublin Castle. That southern wall stood roughly halfway between Christ Church and St Patrick's Cathedrals. So the original Viking town, the embryo from which the city of Dublin emerged, was a tiny place. You can walk the line of the Viking walls today in less than an hour.

Winetavern Street did not assume its modern appearance until the early nineteenth century. By then, its earlier connection to the river had been compromised by the construction of Essex/ Grattan Bridge downstream, which reduced the amount of riverine commerce further upstream. The direct access from the riverside, up the hill to Christ Church, was blocked off by the appearance of a row of houses. When Richmond Bridge was proposed as a replacement for the defunct Ormond Bridge in the early nineteenth century, this obstruction at its southern end was the basis of objections by commercial interests. Moreover, they pointed out that Winetavern Street, as it stood then, was both too steep and too narrow.

The Wide Streets Commissioners tackled the objections with their customary briskness. They knocked down the row of houses, thus opening up the street to the river – and to the new bridge – once again. They widened Winetavern Street to the dimensions it has today, and subsequent building developments and infill from the first half of the nineteenth century gave the street much of its modern appearance.

But still, despite the presence of Christ Church at the top of the street and of the imposing bulk of the Four Courts across the river, the whole area now – fatally – lay west of Capel St/ Essex/Grattan Bridge, which marked the crucial new line of division between east and west. If only just, it was on the wrong side of that line. It is not entirely coincidental that, even in the eighteenth century, the area in the shadow of Christ Church itself was known for its theatres – regarded, with some justice, as loci of dubious morals – and its brothels. Wood Street – between Bride Street and Whitefriar Street – was one of the residences of Peg Plunkett, one of the city's *grandes horizontales*, who styled herself Mrs Leeson and drew the custom of social luminaries such as the viceroy himself, Charles Manners, the Duke of Rutland, whom she referred to affectionately as 'honest Charley'.

Peg Plunkett – Georgian Dublin's most famous brothel madam

Among her other punters was David la Touche, one of the more influential Wide Streets Commissioners; Richard Wellesley, father of the Duke of Wellington; the Earl of Bective; Nathaniel Warren, Lord Mayor of Dublin; and the Duke of Leinster. So Mrs Leeson catered to the appetites of the quality, eschewing randy riff-raff, both in her Wood Street premises and in one of her other houses in Pitt Street, in the more fashionable area just off Grafton Street. It is now renamed Balfe Street in memory of Michael William Balfe, composer of the popular light opera *The Bohemian Girl*, who was born there.[2]

But for all the Mrs Leesons, there were less savoury dens of vice clustered in the old town. Hard by Christ Church was Copper Alley – still there today, but much gentrified – wherein one Dorcas 'Darkey' Kelly kept a brothel rather downmarket of Mrs Leeson's establishments. It was just around the corner from Smock Alley, the city's leading theatre, thus reinforcing the mixture of prejudice and frank observation that associated the stage with the oldest profession. Equally, however, it was not much farther from the New Musick Hall in Fishamble Street, where the first-ever performance of Handel's *Messiah* was given on 13 April 1742. Thus, the still small city centre – although now growing at a dramatic rate – accommodated the sublime and the sordid cheek-by-jowl.

Darkey Kelly was convicted of the murder of one of her punters, a shoemaker, and executed in January 1761, rather gruesomely by first hanging until nearly dead and then finishing the job by burning alive what was left of the poor wretch. Legends grew about her memory, ascribing other murders to her that could not possibly be proved and that are best regarded as retrospective, malicious fictions. But the whole area around Smock Alley was full of brothels. In Smock Alley in 1768, a row in one of them resulted in riots that went on for the best part of a week and resulted in the wholesale wrecking of the suspected premises and were only finally quelled by cavalry.

As with any trading seaport, prostitution had flourished in Dublin for as long as records are extant. In the early seventeenth century, around the time that John Speed was making the first accurate map of the little medieval town, an English soldier called Barnaby Rich complained that 'every filthy alehouse [has] a number of young, idle housewives that are very loathsome, filthy and abominable both in life and manners, and these they call tavern keepers, the most of them known harlots'. Even earlier, we know of the location of certain brothels, one in particular being at the Bagnio Slip (the modern Fownes Street in Temple Bar). The facility in question survived into the eighteenth century.[3]

Attitudes to prostitution depended largely on the disposition of individual magistrates. The severity of the more moral (or moralising) was counterpointed by instances in which judicial leniency could best and most plausibly be explained by the bench having prior acquaintance of the ladies arraigned before them. Brothels and 'massage parlours' have survived in the general Temple Bar area into modern times, as media reports attest, but the modern trade is spread all over the city now and is sustained by the internet and short-term apartment rentals.

Before we return downhill along Winetavern Street, it would be wrong to leave this core of the old Viking town with nothing other than brothels, murders and executions ringing in our ears. For here, within the original walls, stands Christ Church Cathedral, while a short walk along what is first Nicholas Street and then Patrick Street brings you to St Patrick's Cathedral. Christ Church is the Dublin diocesan cathedral of the Church of Ireland; St Patrick's is its national cathedral.

Christ Church is of Viking foundation, St Pat's of Norman. Each is a nineteenth-century confection, one restored to its present condition with whiskey money, the other with beer money. Henry Roe the distiller paid for the remaking of Christ Church, while Sir Benjamin Lee Guinness rendered a similar service to St Pat's. Each was rescued from centuries of neglect and decay, so it's futile to deplore the artificial nature of the restorations as some writers – myself included – have done. After all, Notre-Dame, even before the disastrous fire of 2019, was largely the work of Viollet-le-Duc, another nineteenth-century architect–restorer with the bull-necked confidence of the age: a man who knew what was best.

In the medieval town, the short street that runs west to east towards the end of the gravel ridge that comes in from beyond Kilmainham was the main drag. It was called Skinners Row – it is Christchurch Place today – and contained the Tholsel, an important civic building. 'Tholsel' is a word that has no entry in either the *Oxford English Dictionary* or T.P. Dolan's *Dictionary of Hiberno-English*. It appears to be a uniquely Hiberno-English word, meaning the principal civic building of a town. (The city hall in Kilkenny is still so called; it survives, complete with the ground-floor open arcades typical of eighteenth-century merchants' exchanges.) The name appears to derive from 'Toll Stall' and sounds as if it might be of Viking provenance, although once again there is no entry for it in Diarmaid Ó Muirithe's *From the Viking Word-Hoard: A Dictionary of Scandinavian Words in the Languages of Britain and Ireland*.

The Tholsel combined a number of functions: it was the town hall, where the city fathers deliberated; a merchants'

Fr Mathew Bridge occupies the approximate site that was until 1670
the only urban river crossing on the Liffey.

Constructed in 1648, the Royal Hospital in Kilmainham was the first great monumental building in
the modern city, itself built on the site of the seventh-century monastery of St Maighneann.

Much of the ministry of the Very Rev. Theobald Mathew, the founder of Ireland's Temperance Movement, was dedicated to improving the lot of Ireland's poor.

St Stephen's Green by James Malton.

Portrait of Sarah Fane, Countess of
Westmorland by Ozias Humphrey (1786).
she laid the foundation stone of Islandbridge,
which was originally named for her.

James Gandon's riverine masterpiece, the new
Custom House, pushed the commercial heart of
the city eastward.

In opposition to the gradual eastern and northern development of Dublin,
Islandbridge, first built in 1577, is to the west of Fr Mathew Bridge.

Despite the official moniker Rory O'More bridge, Dubliners have found it very hard to let go of 'Bloody Bridge', which Joyce uses in *Ulysses*.

View from Capel Street looking over the Essex Bridge
(now Grattan Bridge) in the late eighteenth century.

Grattan (Essex) Bridge facilitated the construction of Parliament Street and a new route to the magnificent Parliament House (*above*) via Dame Street.

Grattan Bridge, arguably the most important bridge ever thrown across the Liffey.

The Tholsel, the then equivalent to City Hall, is one of only two buildings featured in Malton's Views of Dublin to not survive into the modern era.

Winetavern Street Bridge to most Dubliners, O'Donovan Rossa Bridge replaced the original Ormond Bridge before it was swept away in a severe storm in 1802.

Mellowes Bridge is the oldest survivor of all the current Liffey Bridges.

If Grattan Bridge divides Dublin east and west, O'Connell Bridge unites it north and south.

Walter Osborne's *Dublin Streets: A Vendor of Books* depicts
a bustling O'Connell Bridge and Aston Quay.

O'Connell Bridge, c. 1960. Car ownership in Dublin rocketed during the sixties.

exchange, including a room for the Trinity Guild of Merchants; a courthouse; and the headquarters of what was Dublin's first attempt at a fire-fighting service. How long it had stood on this site is a matter of dispute. Craig says that it was here, in one form or another, since the early fourteenth century, while Bennett – although agreeing with the fourteenth-century foundation date – locates it first in Winetavern Street and later in High Street. However, both agree that the building on Skinners Row was begun in 1676 and took about seven years to complete. Craig, who showed a sniffy condescension towards merchants and hucksters – he was a gentleman socialist who rather loved his lords – described it as 'typical merchants' architecture, fat and rather complacent, markedly coarser in feeling than any surviving Dublin building'.[4]

Maybe he was on to something beyond prejudice, for the building was not long-lived. Completed, as we saw, in 1683, it lasted barely a hundred years before being abandoned in 1791 and its principal functions dispersed: the city fathers eventually moved to the new city hall, the courts across the river to Gandon's commanding new building and to Green Street Courthouse, the merchants to the new Royal Exchange, and so on. The building was deemed too small for the sundry functions it housed, and moreover, it was in a state of decay to the point where it was a threat to the lives of those within. Its original elaborate cupola shown in a print of 1695 was gone by as early as Brooking's time, suggesting that this top-heavy elaboration was a danger to the structural integrity of the whole building from the very beginning. This all connotes a structure ill-designed and ill-built in the first place. It can hardly be claimed that the site was unsuitable: after all, Christ Church just across the street has stood on similar ground since 1038. At any rate, the Tholsel was eventually demolished in 1809. A small peace park now occupies the site.

The Tholsel is illustrated in Charles Brooking's map of 1728 and most famously by James Malton's engraving of his own watercolour, showing the building in 1791 – just as it was being abandoned. This makes it almost unique among Malton's famous views of classical Dublin at its noonday, being one of only two buildings – the other, the Hibernian Marine School, was located on the lower reaches of the Liffey – not to survive in some shape or form into the modern era.

From here, it's just a short walk downhill along Winetavern Street to reach the bridge and the river. As you do, you pass the civic offices on the right, concerning which there was a furious controversy when they were proposed in the 1970s. The site was archaeologically sensitive: it was at the very heart of the original Viking town, and only heroic excavation work under the direction of Dr Patrick Wallace – later to be director of the National Museum of Ireland – salvaged as much priceless evidence of the earliest urban settlement on the Liffey as it did. The archaeologists should have been given more time. This controversy soured much of public opinion against the buildings put up on the site but in fact – while somewhat sterile, in the manner of so much modern architecture – they sit quite pleasingly by the river on the rising ground. Not everyone agrees with this judgement.

Richmond Bridge remained so called until January 1922 when, in the then customary gust of patriotic onomastics, it was renamed for Jeremiah O'Donovan Rossa. He had been one of the more dubious Fenian patriots, with weaknesses alike for terrorism and alcohol. But none of that stopped Patrick Pearse from delivering his graveside eulogy when Rossa eventually died aged eighty-four in 1915; it was one of the greatest examples of eloquent rhetoric in Irish history and it secured Rossa's place in the nationalist pantheon as nothing else could have done. I imagine that the Duchess of Richmond, by then long in her own grave, was not impressed. But who cares?

– ❀ –

SIX

MELLOWES BRIDGE

MELLOWES BRIDGE WAS a mistake. It was the last of the 'Ormond' bridges built in the 1670s and '80s. Originally built in 1683, it was named – along with the Liffey quay adjacent – for Lord Arran, Ormond's son. The developer was William Ellis, he of the eponymous quay, who owned the land on the north bank and persuaded the city authorities to put up a bridge there. So it was a case of developer-led development which, in this case, misjudged the market.

The reason was that, being the most westerly of the Ormond bridges, upstream of Capel Street and Richmond bridges, it was in the wrong direction. Dublin had begun its inexorable movement to the north and especially to the east. This was the last bridge to be built west of Capel Street for another 145 years until the building of Kingsbridge (Heuston). In that time, the building of both the Ha'penny Bridge and O'Connell Bridge downstream provided the firmest possible proof of the city's *drang nach osten*.

But, as we saw with Bloody Bridge (chapter 3), Ellis – as slippery and opportunist as most of his type – had been granted the land by the river on the north side all the way west of Church Street. So, rather like Sir Humphrey Jervis who developed Capel Street and environs north of his new crossing there, Ellis wished to maximise his return. Unfortunately for him, he was – like Douglas Corrigan's aeroplane years later – going in the wrong direction, for already the direction of travel for the city was establishing itself and there was little comeback for the poor old west.

The bridge that Ellis built was a dud and it fell down in 1763 and had to be rebuilt. The rebuilt version is the one that we see today. That gives it the distinction of being the oldest survivor of all the current Liffey bridges. Craig calls it 'the oldest and one of the most beautiful ... financed by a loan from the La Touche Bank, and built in 1764–8, it is said from the design of General Charles Vallancey, who was then an engineer in the Ordnance Office. He later attained an unenviable fame as a speculative and wrong-headed antiquary, but for this bridge with its niches and its judicious rustication we would forgive him much.'[1]

As with so much developer-led urban development then and since, it may have made sense to William Ellis. Note how sedulously he ingratiated himself with his patron Ormond by naming the bridge for his patron's son, before deftly shifting his allegiance to Tyrconnell a few years later when there was radical regime change upon the accession of James II to the throne. But what was good for Ellis was not necessarily good for Dublin, for the reason just stated.

To this day, it is one of those bridges from nowhere to nowhere. Well, almost. The rebuilt bridge was named for Queen Charlotte, wife of King George III, who had come to the throne around eight years earlier and would stay there for another fifty-two years until 1820. To be fair, the north side of the river, under Ellis's

Queen's Bridge with Home's Hotel and Usher's Quay on the left (1837)

superintendence and that of Jervis a little to the east, was developing rapidly and was a busy quarter, all part of that easting process downstream of Bloody Bridge that we have already acknowledged.

By the time of the rebuilding, it was increasingly clear that Capel Street Bridge was the key line of demarcation and that areas on the wrong side of it – that is, upstream to the west – were on the losing side of the process. Still, it was not an absolute process. The southern bank of the Liffey at this point never developed the sort of quickening urbanity increasingly common downstream, but it was not completely inert, either, as we shall see.

Back on the north side, Queen Street gives access to the bridge and also its name in common Dublin parlance. The street is named for Catherine of Braganza, the wife of King Charles II, and not – as one might think – for George III's missus for whom the bridge was renamed after the rebuilding of 1768. So while dear old Queen Charlotte has nearly but not entirely been written out of urban history, Liam Mellowes, the republican revolutionary for whom it is now officially named, has never quite been written into it. As usual, no one calls it by its official name and not one person in a thousand could tell you accurately which of the bridges on the Liffey is named for Mellowes. I certainly couldn't until I began to research this book. But if you had said Queen Street Bridge, I'd have had it straight off – if only because I was nearly marmelised there one evening by an articulated truck crashing a red light. Queen Street almost certainly represents the terminus of one of the ancient pre-urban roads converging on Dublin. Three of them appear to have reached the river at or about this point, in order to give access to the nearby ford and therefore to the south shore. The same may be said of Blackhall Place (see chapter 17) parallel to it and just to the west.

Queen Street itself dates from the 1660s, when this part of Oxmantown Green was first divided into lots for further development, which is what gave the indefatigable William Ellis his start. It is short but it gives access to the west side of Smithfield, one of the greatest open spaces in a city not exactly over endowed with them. This entire district was rationally planned: Queen Street – ramrod straight as fashion demanded, to contrast with twisting medieval lanes – was to be the equivalent of Capel Street. But that did not fully materialise, because whereas Capel Street met the eastern end of North King Street and effected a junction with the western end of Drumcondra Lane (later renamed Dorset Street) and therefore access to the principal exit from the city to the north, Queen Street came to a dead end when it met North King Street further to the west, set to be the northern boundary of urban expansion for the moment.

Queen Street looking south across the river is clearly orientated on St Catherine's Church, up the hill at Thomas Street. Or perhaps it might be more accurate to say that the church was centred on Queen Street, which already existed when St Catherine's was built in 1769. While not a dramatic building, although a pleasing one, it offers a natural perspective point for Queen Street looking south. This habit of orientation on perspective points was one of the distinguishing features of all classical and Enlightenment urban development, seen at its finest – in Dublin, anyway – in the wonderful vista along Merrion Square South and Upper Mount Street to St Stephen's Church, the Pepper Canister in popular parlance, at Mount Street Crescent.

Craig makes the point about St Catherine's that it was intended by its architect, John Smyth, to have a spire that would have represented a more dramatic perspective point for Queen Street. But, as he notes acerbically, it 'was never built and the temporary hat placed over the stump [of the tower] is still there, after nearly two hundred years'.[2] It's still there seventy more years after Craig wrote about it.

In a sense, Queen Street and Blackhall Place, running parallel to it and a little to the west, form joint western boundaries for the developing city. They are the principal north–south axes in this part of town. Just to the east of Queen Street is the great open space of Smithfield and, at a right-angle to it adjacent, the smaller space of Haymarket. Significantly, a proposal to build a palace for the Duke of Ormond at the western end of these Oxmantown lands was never executed, marking a further decline in the area's prestige. A Viceregal palazzo in the area would surely have helped to arrest its later decline.

However, Smithfield, which appears to have taken its name from the London equivalent, became a great open market for the trading of farm animals and provisions. Instead of a ducal display space, commerce dominated. And not just agricultural commerce. With the jobbers, dealers and drovers came the attendant retinues of grog shops, whores and thieves, all this profane foregathering taking place practically at the back of St Paul's RC parish church (1835–7) that faced onto Arran Quay and the river, a sober, restrained and discreet contrast to the doings at the rear. Smithfield is a magnificent open piazza whose potential as an urban display space has been squandered: imagine what any Italian town would have made of such an opportunity! Aristocrats would have been tripping over each other to live here. Instead, Dublin offered only two centuries of cow shit and, latterly, an unedifying horse fair on Sunday mornings.

From the beginning, when it was first laid out in the seventeenth century, Smithfield was designated a market area. It was towards the eastern end of Oxmantown Green, whose whole extent was to be taken in by the burgeoning urban development that followed. A bowling green was laid out for the benefit of the quality a little further west to lend some tone – what's left of it is now the gardens of the Law Society (formerly the Blue Coat School) on Blackhall Place. As we have seen, Ormond never built his putative palazzo hereabouts. What was built instead, in 1702, was the massive Royal Barracks (now part of the National Museum of Ireland), capable of housing 12,000 troops when fully occupied. David Dickson remarks that in 1665 'there was a well-defined cluster of high-status families in residence' in the general area, but subsequent developments quickly diminished its allure.[3]

Because Smithfield, the most conspicuous space in the district, was from its earliest days given over to commerce and trade, it lessened its attractions for prestige residential purposes. This was compounded by the arrival of the barracks adjacent, for both men and horses were catered for there: the men had their raucous and unsophisticated requirements attended to and the horses were fed, all in and from the plaza whose character was already firmly established. It would continue in this shabby vein until the early twenty-first century. The barracks dominated the area: it is the oldest inhabited barracks in Europe and was the largest cavalry barracks in the British Isles. Being to the west of Capel Street, this part of Dublin was ever less attractive to fashion anyway, as the process of northing and easting began its relentless march, the whole thing not helped by the near conjunction of the barracks and Smithfield.

On the threshold of its golden century, Dublin was a sort of cross between a wannabe Urbino and Dodge City. Crime was a major problem and the maintenance of law and order an equal one. We have already seen the sort of trouble that attended the brothels in the lee of Christ Church and the annual riots between gangs of weavers from the Liberties and the Ormond Boys from the markets near Smithfield. That wasn't the half of it.

In addition to lower-class lawlessness, there was upper-class lawlessness. Dickson summarises this phenomenon. There was 'brazen upper-class delinquency: a set of young bucks known as the "pinking dindies", many of them connected with Trinity College, became notorious for roughing up brothel-keepers, gamblers and were "single men and citizens who neither wore fine clothes [n]or swords"'.[4] Being children of privilege, they were effectively beyond the law.

What resources did the eighteenth-century city, growing with all the urgency of a frontier town and plainly exhibiting some of the manners and mores one might expect in such a locale, possess against these various disturbing infractions? Not much, and not nearly enough. There was no police force in any modern sense, nor would there be until the formation of the Peace Preservation force in 1814, and even then only a shadow force, although it later evolved in 1836 into the (Royal) Irish Constabulary and the Dublin Metropolitan Police. In the eighteenth century, there were only parish watches, local men who kept a lookout for trouble but whose powers, feeble as they were, did not extend beyond whatever civil (i.e., Church of Ireland) parish they represented. This meant that a criminal only had to cross the parish boundary to be in the clear. Ultimately, responsibility for the maintenance of law and order rested with the lord mayor and senior city officials. They alone had the power to summon troops if things got bad – which they often did: there was a constant fear of riots by disgruntled journeymen and other lower-class elements – and they did so with the greatest reluctance and, it might be said, not often enough.

As for Smithfield and environs, an attempt was finally made to improve the area as late as 1997. Competitions were held for urban renewal projects, and over the next decade the plaza did indeed change character and took on many of the virtues of sensible urban planning. This was helped by a growing gentrification in the general area as the Celtic Tiger began to bare its teeth. One of the consequences was a huge increase in house prices – all, of course, to end in disaster in 2008 – which obliged young professionals with skills but sans serious money to move to areas previously regarded as unfashionable. In the case of Smithfield, this was particularly marked in the Stoneybatter and Manor Street areas adjacent – and in the side streets off them – which became a new locus of bobo* cool. It is full of wine bars, food shops, stylish but

---

* 'Bourgeois bohemian' – a coinage originally minted by the American writer David Brooks to describe a new middle class, not conspicuously wealthy but embracing post-traditional pubs, restaurants and so on. In a generation, it has become a centre of modish delights.

As for the plaza itself, although vastly improved, it has never lived up to the original hopes of the public planners, well and all as they have done. There was, of course, inflated talk and windy aspirations, mostly from politicians and not from the planners who tended to be more restrained and realistic. But at the start of the process of renewal, a government minister of the time expressed the hope that the new Smithfield might become the Times Square of Dublin – helpfully adding that Smithfield was about the same size as the Piazza Navona in Rome![5]

Alas, it was not to be. Not quite. It was the old story: too far west. They built and renewed but the punters did not come, at least not in anything like the numbers required to fulfil the more optimistic hopes. But for a place like Smithfield as it was, isn't it better to aim high even if you fall short? Dublin has many able administrators and planners, but insufficient dreamers.

Almost fourteen years to the day after the minister's burst of optimism, the *Irish Times* was reporting in a more melancholy and restrained manner about Smithfield in a report that opened: 'It was supposed to be a bustling cultural quarter but instead it's seen as a barren, intimidating place.'[6] In the interim between the two reports, the Celtic Tiger had expired and all construction and renewal projects, including *grands projets* like Smithfield, had either stopped or been put on hold or, at a minimum, been severely cut back. It's fair to say that the hope to create a new, magnetic civic centre has not been realised and looks as if it never will be. But Smithfield, although wide open and rather bleak, especially in

---

1960s counter-cultural values. You can measure out the bobo hangouts not so much in coffee spoons as in coffee shops.

St Catherine's Church c. 1799, one of James Malton's famous views of Dublin

bad weather, which is not unknown in Dublin's fair city, is vastly improved on the shabby shambles it was before the renewal. Alas, the wretched horse fair is still there on the first Sunday of every month as a reminder of 'de rare oul' times'.

On the south side, Queen's Street Bridge gives access to the quays and Heuston Station and roads west out of town. It also gives onto Bridgefoot Street, straight ahead, which takes you up to the junction with Thomas Street opposite St Catherine's Church – famous probably more than anything else for being the building outside which the patriot and spectacularly inept revolutionary Robert Emmet was hanged and decapitated after his farcical 'rising' of 1803. It points you towards the Liberties, the south-western inner suburbs of the old town. Liberties were medieval areas not subject to the direct control of the lord mayor and town authorities. Instead, local power was devolved to bigwigs who effectively had palatinate jurisdiction – that is, autonomous powers to raise revenue and enforce rules. The principal liberties, all contiguous in this area, were that of St Sepulchre, belonging to the archbishop of Dublin, and the liberties of Donore and of the abbey of St Thomas.

The abbey of St Thomas was dissolved in the carnival of vandalism under the boor Henry VIII known to history as the dissolution of the monasteries; Donore was bundled in with it. The liberty was granted to one William Brabazon, a man on the make who had the cynical good sense to stay on the right side of the new regime and whose descendants went on to prosper as the earls of Meath. Thus the Liberties *tout court* are often referred to as the earl of Meath's Liberties.

Of Bridgefoot Street that leads you uphill from Queen Street Bridge to this junction opposite St Catherine's, there is little to say. It is not, to understate the point, a feast for the eye. You wouldn't confuse it with Florence.

All in all, the bridge now named for Liam Mellowes turned out to be something of a wrong turn up a cul-de-sac. It was too far west, and while it contributed in the short-term to the development of its north-side environs, on the south side it accessed an area that is interesting and lively but that has never been fashionable. Instead, by the time the bridge was rebuilt in 1768 the famous northing and easting was blowing like a hurricane.

All the urgent action of the city was moving downriver, and the early developments of the Georgian city were established on the gently rising ground to the north, centred on the Gardiner estate and Sackville Street. And Sackville Street – much later to be renamed O'Connell Street – led at its southern end to the next bridge to which we turn: O'Connell Bridge.

— ❀ —

SEVEN

O'CONNELL BRIDGE

O'CONNELL BRIDGE IS your only man. If Capel Street Bridge divides the city east and west, this unites it north and south. It is the principal river crossing of the modern city. The north-side–south-side dichotomy is now so dominant in the public imagination that it is all too easy to dismiss it as flim-flam, pointing out earnestly (and repeatedly or incessantly, as the present work does) that it is the east–west division that really matters. It is, but that does not mean that the north-side–south-side divide is of no account.

For a start, if you cross the bridge from south to north having come down from St Stephen's Green, say, you notice almost immediately the deterioration of the public fabric. This is especially true to the north of O'Connell Street in the various streets leading off the main drag. The north inner city, from the river to the Royal Canal, is an embarrassing shambles. The urban centre possesses no other area as large in which are concentrated buildings and streets of such depressing ugliness, with hardly anything in the way of architectural distinction to lift the human spirit. (An honourable and noble exception: Croke Park, the headquarters of the Gaelic Athletic Association, is a masterpiece.)

The story of the district, running east of Capel Street up to Mountjoy Square, with O'Connell Street as its central axis and showcase, is to a large extent the story of the Gardiner clan. The original of the species was Luke Gardiner (*c.* 1690–1755), a Dubliner of unknown but modest origins who was one of those people who seemed to come from nowhere in the wake of the Williamite victory and the great Protestant stability that followed, equipped with nothing much more than a talent for commerce and making money. Speaker Conolly of the Irish parliament, a generation older than Gardiner, who had built for himself and his family the greatest of all Irish classical houses, Castletown, just west of the city, modelled on the Palazzo Farnese in Rome, was another – and reckoned the richest man in Ireland.

Gardiner appears to have made his money in property development, for which he had – and bequeathed – a real talent, and banking. This was fortified by a good marriage to Anne Stewart, daughter of Hon. Alexander Stewart who was the son of William Stewart, 1st viscount Mountjoy. She was also related to the earls of Blessington, so the marriage was successful both socially and materially.

His early money came from various public offices and he became an admired state official. But his *métier* was property development. By 1729 he had taken ownership of almost all of the estate centred on the old St Mary's Abbey, giving him a firm foothold on what were then the eastern margins of the expanding city. He went on to be the principal developer of this new north-east quadrant. His first major development was Henrietta Street, huge houses on a short street off Bolton Street, which is the point where Capel Street, pushing west, meets the southern end of Drumcondra Lane/Dorset Street, pointing north out of Dublin.

These Henrietta Street houses were larger than anything subsequently built in Georgian Dublin. From this beginning, his development interests billowed out. He built up Upper Dorset Street, Rutland/Parnell Square and Drogheda Lane, having bought these lands from Sir Humphrey Jervis in 1714, Jervis having previously bought out the Moore/Drogheda interest. He turned the lane into a street – the very finest in contemporary Dublin – and renamed it Sackville Street, after Lionel Sackville, 1st duke of Dorset, the lord lieutenant. Rutland Square was a co-development with Bartholomew Mosse, the entrepreneur who in 1757 opened the very first dedicated maternity hospital in the British Isles at the top of Drogheda Lane/Sackville Street. It was and is a building of distinction, designed by Richard Cassels, the finest architect in Dublin prior to Gandon. By then, Gardiner was dead but his development of Sackville Street, adjacent to the Rotunda, was complete. It was wide and spacious but extended only as far as Henry Street; then narrowed down to the river, where there was a ferry to go across to the southern bank. In the middle of the new Sackville Street, he enclosed a long rectangular walkway, where the quality could do a kind of *passeggiata* of an evening.

Lower Sackville Street was not widened to the same width as the upper part of the street until 1784, and with this widening the pressure to bridge the Liffey at its end-point became ever more urgent. It was a proposal that, in one form or another, had been lying around for a while. It invariably met with the hostility of vested interests, who knew perfectly well and quite correctly that any such bridge would be critical in pushing the heart of the city even further to the east and away from Capel Street Bridge. The usual mercantile interests, well represented on the city assembly, were comfortable with existing arrangements and had no desire to see them disturbed.

This assembly, later to mutate into the Dublin Corporation, was a survivor from the medieval town. It was representative but in no modern sense was it remotely democratic. That was an idea that lay far away in the unimaginable future. Those it represented were freemen of the city, comprising aldermen – consisting of forty-eight men originally nominated by the twenty-four-man medieval town council and their successors – who in turn nominated a further ninety-six, most of whom were members of influential guilds.[1] It was, and remained, a closed shop.

The key development that finally prompted the building of the bridge was the removal of the Custom House from Essex Quay, upriver and adjacent to Capel Street Bridge (on the site of the present Clarence Hotel), downriver to its present site at what was then the eastern end of the Liffey quays. The Custom House was the centre of Dublin commerce, although an increasingly inefficient and unsatisfactory one; it was clear that a fixed bridge downstream – remember that, at this time, there was no bridged crossing point on the Liffey downriver of Capel Street – would impede riverine traffic from any further passage upstream and fundamentally change the city's economic geography.

This accounted for the vicious opposition to the new Custom House, which eventually opened for business in 1791. In the ten years antecedent, however, the opposition to what became the most distinguished building in the city was formidable and continuous. It was claimed that this drained, swampy land belonged to the city and that therefore building on the site was illegal. This was disputed: the site was also, conveniently, claimed by John Claudius Beresford, the most influential figure in the Irish administration of the late eighteenth century. He was, in turn, accused of feathering his own nest by encouraging the development.

Beresford, connected to the powerful family of the marquess of Waterford, was among other things a member of the Wide Streets Commission. This body of enlightened and often self-interested bullies had been founded in 1757 and presided over the creation of straight, wide streets – true to their name – in place of the twisted warren of lanes that had characterised the medieval town. To them we owe the dimensions of the great Georgian streets and squares: O'Connell Street, Westmoreland and D'Olier Streets, Nassau Street and many more. They were a top-down, authoritarian clique in a manner emblematic of a pre-democratic age, but they got things done while brushing aside special pleading by vested interests – other than their own, of course. Collectively, they were the nearest thing Dublin ever saw or ever will see to a Baron Haussmann, another enlightened bully who took no nonsense.

The opposition to the new Liffey bridge had been of long standing. As far back as 1753, one Gilbert Allason, a notary public, was appointed by the city assembly to prepare the case for opposing any such bridge. He wrote 'if it be at present inconvenient that the Custom House is so far from the Exchange, how much greater will be the inconvenience when a new Custom House shall (as it must) be built below the new Bridge? And to whom will this inconvenience be greater than to persons so fat, so unwieldy as the Aldermen?'[2] But the final move of the Custom House settled the matter and threw the design of the new bridge open to competition.

Carlisle Bridge with the Custom House in the background, c. 1800

It was finally won by Gandon, an earlier proposal from whom had been rejected as too expensive; his revised proposal was accepted in 1789. Beresford laid the foundation stone in 1791 and the bridge opened four years later.

The bridge was named for Frederick Howard, 5th earl of Carlisle, an earlier lord lieutenant to whom Beresford had been close. It was to retain this name until 1880. Carlisle Bridge was a three-span masonry structure, narrower than the recently widened Lower Sackville Street. Balustraded parapets tapered elegantly at the four corners to create the narrowing. From early days, however, there were problems. It was in need of structural repair from as early as 1818. As for the narrowing, the carriageway – at only 13 metres wide – soon proved too cramped for the weight of vehicular traffic that it quickly attracted, all the more because of the crucial role it played in opening up the route from the river to College Green, the university and the magnificent old parliament house.

The opening of that route was probably the single most important development in the making of the modern city. The entire spinal axis of Dublin was now moved decisively and irrevocably downriver to the east, away from the medieval hub and the Capel Street area adjacent, so that the spine soon ran from Dorset Street, via North Frederick Street/Cavendish Row and Sackville Street, over the Carlisle Bridge and into Westmoreland Street, thus accessing College Green and, from there, Grafton Street – and the various new centres of fashion off it – to St Stephen's Green. Grafton Street had first been laid out in the early eighteenth century but in its modern form is a nineteenth-century makeover, part of the process just described. That spinal route remains the central axis of modern Dublin. Any attempts to further re-orientate the city, either east – as in the late twentieth and early twenty-first centuries – or west, as we saw with Smithfield, have not disturbed this basic urban geography.

These streets were all either developed or redeveloped in the early years of the nineteenth century. D'Olier Street and Westmoreland Street – the latter the key link to College Green – had been in contemplation and various stages of planning since the 1790s at least, but the usual wrangles delayed their beginning. This can be seen from their names, already somewhat anachronistic by the time the work was actually completed: one is for Jeremiah D'Olier, city sheriff in 1790; the other for John Fane, 10th earl of Westmorland, lord lieutenant (inevitably) back in 1790–4, at least ten years before the street was laid out.

There is an interesting detail in the spelling of the street name and that of the lord lieutenant's title. The street name contains an additional 'e' in the middle, accounting for its Irish pronunciation: West-MORE-land, whereas Johnny Fane's title was rendered in the English manner, similar to the now archaic county name from which it derived, Westmorland, which is still pronounced like that, West'mland, on the other side. Really, the English know nothing.

At any rate, at the end of the street, just as it was about to yield to College Green, Gandon designed his magnificent new eastern entrance to the parliament house, to give ready access to the House of Lords. This superb portico, comprising six pillars reaching over the footpath to the edge of the carriageway with Corinthian orders of decoration aloft, was one of the most successful additions imaginable to a building already of the greatest architectural distinction. This was done in the heady days of the 1780s and 1790s.

Westmoreland and D'Olier Streets were the last major urban project superintended by the Wide Streets Commissioners. In one sense, the Act of Union (1801) rendered them redundant, since all forms of Irish local government and governance were now at a discount. In another sense, however, it was simply that their best work was done. As early as 1762, they had punched Parliament Street through south from Capel Street Bridge to Dame Street: it was the same width as the bridge. As to Dame Street, it was widened down to the parliament house from 1769. In aggregate, the great wide quadrilateral of Parliament Street/Dame Street/ Westmoreland Street and the south quays embraces this vital city quarter, now distinguished as the rather hectic area called Temple Bar. It's easy to deplore aspects of modern Temple Bar – too many pubs is the usual moan – but for anyone who remembers the sad state of neglect into which the area had been allowed to fall prior to the redevelopment in the 1980s and '90s, it has been a model of how a city might be remade. The post-medieval street pattern has been preserved for the most part, albeit girdled by the commissioners' work. Then Taoiseach Charlie Haughey was a crook, but he wasn't all bad: this would not have happened without his imprimatur.

As to the Carlisle Bridge itself, it survived in its original form, as Gandon had designed it, for the best part of a century. Then, its inherent flaws and problems forced the issue. Not the least of its shortcomings was its number of traffic accidents, with many pedestrians coming to a grisly end under the hooves of galloping horses. The problems had been identified as early as the 1830s but not until the 1860s was the Dublin Corporation in a position to announce a competition for the design of a replacement. This attracted more than forty entries. Then the winning entry was not accepted, however. At this point the quickening pulse of Irish nationalism was felt. On 8 August 1864, the foundation stone for the O'Connell Monument was laid by Lord Mayor Peter Paul McSwiney. It was the masterwork of the great Irish Victorian sculptor John Henry Foley and was formally unveiled on 15 August 1882.

In the meantime, the matter of the bridge itself had been settled at last. The ratepayers had argued for years – with the provincial parsimony typical of that sad era in the city's life – that they should not have to shoulder the financial burden. They looked to the imperial treasury, which did not meet their gaze. Instead, the Dublin Port and Docks Board – recently established, the latest of a number of successive local authorities charged with the superintendence of the city's maritime commerce – took the

The laying of the foundation stone of the O'Connell Monument, *Illustrated London News*, 1864

matter in hand. Its chief engineer, Bindon Blood Stoney, was charged with the task, and it was he who produced the design that we have today. The Port and Docks Board retained the name of Carlisle Bridge and even inscribed it into the stonework. But the corporation, now firmly in nationalist hands at a time of rising nationalist temperature, had the final word. O'Connell Bridge it became, with the board's lapidary inscription covered up with the metal plates which you can still see on the bridge and which read:

CARLISLE BRIDGE
BUILT 1794
REBUILT BY THE DUBLIN PORT AND DOCKS
BOARD
RENAMED
O'CONNELL
BY THE MUNICIPAL COUNCIL, 1880
RIGHT HONBLE EDMUND DWYER GRAY MP
LORD MAYOR
JAMES W. MACKEY, KT DL HIGH SHERIFF
BINDON B. STONEY, ENGINEER
W.J. DOHERTY, CONTRACTOR

This is not the only inscription on O'Connell Bridge. On the west side of the bridge, atop the balustrade towards the corner of Bachelors Walk, there is another one. The wording reads, in full:

THIS PLAQUE COMMEMORATES
FR. PAT NOISE
ADVISOR TO PEADAR CLANCEY.
HE DIED UNDER SUSPICIOUS
CIRCUMSTANCES WHEN HIS
CARRIAGE PLUNGED INTO THE
LIFFEY ON AUGUST 10TH 1919.
ERECTED BY THE HSTI

As with everything, there is a story at the back of this, none of it having anything to do with Fr Pat Noise. It is this.

In 1996, Dublin City Council resolved on a 'project' to mark the forthcoming millennium. So they ordered up a digital countdown clock, dropping it into the waters of the Liffey at this point, where it was to be an object of wonder to the gawping citizenry until it dutifully counted down the time to midnight on 31 December 1999/1 January 2000. (The fact that the actual millennial change was not properly for a further year, until 31 December 2000/1 January 2001, was pointed out by some pedants whose entreaties were very properly ignored.)

Up on the bridge, meanwhile, a control mechanism was set for the clock in case things went awry and adjustments were required. With comic predictability, they did. The clock was in the river but very soon the river was in the clock. The Liffey, never the cleanest stream in Christendom, deposited a persistent sludge on the clock face, which made it difficult to read. Other woes attended it, and no sooner was it in the river than it was out again for repairs, adjustments and what have you.

The clock did not even see out the year 1996, let alone make it to the millennium where all sorts of showbiz hoopla had been planned as the clock ticked down to what irreverent Dubliners called the aluminium. After sundry fumblings and fiddlings with the works, the engineers admitted defeat; the clock never returned to the Liffey water, and the control box aloft on the balustrade was redundant. It was removed, leaving a small declivity in the stonework to mark its brief presence there.

Enter the plaque as above. Person or persons unknown had fashioned a commemorative plaque to the exact dimensions of the control box and surreptitiously placed it in the declivity, all very neat. Dublin City Council, swollen with aldermanic hubris, ordered its removal in 2007 as it was *unauthorised*. (The horror: pearls were clutched in the city offices.) It was duly removed, only to be replaced by a facsimile. This time, the political mood had changed: a councillor named Dermot Lacey, a human being with a sense of humour and of the ridiculous, lobbied hard for the retention of Noise. Pressure duly came on to leave the Noise memorial *in situ*, which was done. So there it sits to this day.

It is a hoax. Pat Noise never existed. He is a fiction. Peadar Clancey [*sic*] most certainly was not. He was second-in-command of the Dublin Brigade of the IRA during the war of independence and was executed, while being held prisoner, as a reprisal for the IRA's actions on Bloody Sunday, 21 November 1921. He was 'shot while trying to escape', the usual feeble military lie for cold-blooded murder. Later, after independence, the army barracks at Islandbridge – since sold off for housing development – was renamed in his honour.

A hint as to the inauthenticity of the plaque is that Clancy's surname was misspelt the first time round and the error repeated a second time. There was also the matter of the sponsoring body. No one had a clue as to what HSTI stood for, although some suspected that it might be an anagram. Inevitably, ballads – those excuses for music to which Irish people appear to be incurably addicted – were written (and, worse, sung) about Pat Noise and his deeds of derring-do. Noise about Noise. Anyway, the plaque is there for good and all now and has become a little part of the city's fabric. The identity of the mysterious donors has never been revealed, but you have to hand it to them: they are the HSTI.

O'Connell Bridge is now the same width as Lower O'Connell Street and is one of the widest bridges in Europe. It looks almost square but in fact is a few metres wider than it's long. When Lower Sackville Street, as it then was, was widened to its present extent in 1784, it changed the nature of the street. What the first Luke Gardiner had built in Upper Sackville Street was a harmonious series of elegant houses for the wealthy. There was not a hint of commerce there. The widening of Drogheda Lane to become Lower Sackville Street introduced commerce to the street for the first time, a process that accelerated as the nineteenth century went on. Moreover, the whole tenor of the street changed. At the southern end of Gardiner's development, where the old street had narrowed, two new structures were erected which gave an entirely new focus and definition to O'Connell Street.

The first was Nelson Pillar. It was a granite column set in the middle of the street in 1809, with a statue of the victor of Trafalgar aloft. The victory marked the apogee of British naval power, at least in purely military terms, and was a moment of patriotic pride in British hearts. Ireland, however, although formally joined in union with the larger island, was rapidly developing a nationalist temper, one that waxed as the century went on. Public feeling about Nelson was, shall we say, equivocal. James Joyce, a nationalist but not a republican, has his *alter ego*, Stephen Dedalus, refer to Nelson in *Ulysses* as 'the onehandled adulterer', a reference to the fact that Nelson had lost an arm in an earlier naval battle and had been conducting an affair in Naples with Lady Emma Hamilton.

For years, a pointless debate about who should replace Horatio on top of the Pillar went on, candidates including Jesus Christ and Patrick Pearse. Nothing was done, however, until the IRA – considered to be not dead but sleeping – blew the whole thing up in March 1966, the golden anniversary year of the Easter Rising. It was an appropriate commemorative act for such an outfit – actually, it was the work of a freelance republican maverick – and to be fair to them, they did a very professional job. Despite the potential for havoc in blowing up a tall granite pillar, even in the small hours of the morning, it was a very neat job. No one was hurt. When the Irish army came along later to remove the stump, which was all that was left of it, they blew out three-quarters of the windows in O'Connell Street.

For all people's ambiguity about the pillar, it had stood there, slap in the middle of the city's main street, for 157 years. It was the city's principal meeting point – 'see you at the pillar' – and the point of departure for the tram service. It was a landmark; in time, even people who had no care for Nelson or his memory came to have a sentimental regard for the old thing. The site stood blank for years after the explosion and again various replacement options were canvassed. Eventually, the Spire replaced it: a tall (very tall) tapering needle in stainless steel designed by the British architect Ian Ritchie was finally installed in 2003. It has never quite matched the old pillar in public affection or as a meeting place, nor does the public transport system – now mainly buses – use it as a terminus. While it divides opinion, I think it very elegant and beautiful. It has been the central, indispensable feature in the much-needed renewal of the street, which has been partially successful: only by its dimensions can O'Connell Street any longer be considered Dublin's principal thoroughfare or centre of urban activity. The other thing about the Spire is its abstraction: it's not *about* anything in particular. It entails no didactic finger-jabbing about this dead hero or that. It is simply itself.

The other early nineteenth-century structure that changed the nature of Luke Gardiner's street was the General Post Office, perhaps the finest monumental achievement of Francis Johnston, the leading Irish architect in the decades after Gandon. Like Gandon's House of Lords, its portico is supported by six classical pillars reaching over the pavement. The building dominated the entire streetscape from the moment it was inaugurated in January

1818. It was, of course, the principal republican garrison in the Easter Rising of 1916 and was badly damaged by British artillery, although fully restored by 1932.

Sackville/O'Connell Street was the centrepiece of the Gardiner estate, the first such coherent, rational development in the city's history. Later it was to be eclipsed by the two great south-side urban estates, those of Merrion and Fitzwilliam. But Gardiner was first, and he was first for a reason. He was in early – as early as 1713 he was acquiring land on the southern bank of the river, downriver of what is now O'Connell Bridge. But the legacy of the Gardiners lay across the river. One authority puts it with simple clarity: 'the history of the Gardiner estate is the history of Dublin's north side'.[3] One key reason for this early north-side development was topography: the ground rises gently from the river on this side. It is uphill all the way from the river to Mountjoy Square, the highest and most easterly part of the estate, above any possible flood line. This was a very material consideration in the later fashionable south-east quadrant: the swampy ground inhibited its development without, as we shall soon see, arresting it.

Luke Gardiner the first, patriarch of the dynasty, was acquiring land on the north side from 1714. He developed Henrietta Street, as we have seen, and the streets surrounding it. There were other, smaller holdings within the overall Gardiner empire – Archdall around what is now North Great George's Street, Dominick around the street that still bears the name, and Eccles in the north-west corner where the street, home to Leopold Bloom, likewise bears the name. But these were islands in the Gardiner sea, which encompassed most of what lay east of Rutland/Parnell Square across to Mountjoy Square and practically down to the river. It is no accident that the principal north–south axis in the eastern part of the development is called Gardiner Street to this day, although – like much of the Gardiner development – history and what Yeats much later called 'the dull spite of this unmannerly town' have not been kind to it. Then there are other streets, no better treated by time and fate, which bear names related to the Gardiners: Blessington Street and Mountjoy Square to take two obvious examples.

But in its day, which occupied most of the eighteenth century, this was the area for new wealth to display itself. Even today, walking the area in its scandalously decayed state, you can immediately reconstruct mentally the beauty and harmony of the original. At its apex, begun as late as 1792 and not finished until 1818, stood Mountjoy Square, the nearest thing to a mathematical square in the Georgian city; the two great south-side squares, Merrion and Fitzwilliam, are rectangles, as is St Stephen's Green, while Parnell Square is a rhombus, an irregular quadrilateral.

An informal census conducted by a heroic Anglican clergyman, Rev. James Whitelaw, in 1798 – one of the truly great and shamefully forgotten Dubliners – revealed the success of the Gardiner estate. It had already established itself by showing one of the highest concentrations of wealth in any city district, including the very telling, and very high, figure for the number of servants per 100 residents: 93.2. This was endorsed by *Watson's Dublin Almanack*, published in the same fateful year as Whitelaw's census. It tracked the homes of peers and members of parliament and found a big concentration in the Gardiner estate, now matching or surpassing fashionable areas on the south side which had established themselves in the second half of the century.[4]

At the close of the century, around the time of the Act of Union, the city had its wealth pretty evenly distributed on either side of the river; although, as a persistent pattern was asserting itself, the north-west quadrant was a back marker: many ambitious development plans for that area were never realised. None the less, the modern dichotomy of wealth and prestige was not there in the Georgian city: there was money on both sides of the river. The fact that the Gardiner estate, the original of the species, was allowed to fall into such a state of decay from about 1850 on was – and remains – a stain on Dublin's reputation and *amour propre*. One might shout at the city authorities, as Ciaran Fitzgerald, captain of the Irish rugby team, once bawled at his pack during a crunch game at Lansdowne Road against England: 'Where's your pride? Where's your fuckin' pride?!' (It worked: Ireland won that match, en route to the triple crown in 1982; but the north inner city of Dublin is still a shambles.)

That part of the city requires a bolt of municipal socialism. Only a public, state-driven and planned renewal can restore or, better, replace what has been lost. Nowhere do you look up and see anything that lifts the human spirit, just arse-patching architecture, cheap and throwaway. There is no point in hoping that the market offers any kind of solution here. It can't: developers are in business for profit – quite right, too – but they can have neither unified ambition nor desire for shabby areas like this. It's not their job. They make their money elsewhere: let them away. So what is needed is something top-down, like the Wide Streets Commissioners or Baron Haussmann or the man from the ministry who knows best. The legacy of the tenement slums, the worst temporal features of which have been happily erased, persists here in the absence of vision, of ambition, of desire. Where's your fuckin' pride, Dublin, that you can let this visual smorgasbord of mediocrity and ugliness subsist where once was classical harmony and reason? It's tragic, and all practically within pissing distance of O'Connell Street. Oh, how we need dreamers and lunatics.

It isn't as if we are poor any more. That excuse no longer washes.

The south-east quadrant, as is well-known, was established from the 1740s onwards, the anchor point being the Earl (later Duke) of Leinster's decision to build his town house there: Leinster House. As he had said it would, fashion followed, and soon the area east of St Stephen's Green, encompassing the Merrion and Fitzwilliam estates, became the chic quarter of the city, as it has remained ever since.

Although well-known, the statement that Leinster House started the rush to the south-east requires some qualification, simply based on the evidence. The push either side of Grafton Street was not entirely dependent on the Earl of Leinster, although his grand house was a huge accelerant in a process already in train, if slowly. To the east of Grafton Street, Dawson Street – named for Joshua Dawson, the entrepreneur who developed much of this area – was already in place by the first decade of the eighteenth century; its most notable building, then as now, the Mansion House, dates from as early as 1714, contemporaneous with the development of Grafton Street. Molesworth Street, pushing further east from Dawson Street, was first laid out in the 1720s, again well before the building of the earl's house. But Leinster House was, none the less, the key development; Kildare Street followed and then came the huge Georgian squares and streets – Merrion Square et al. – further east again.

Still, it was all an improbable development, as the area was low lying and prone to flooding. Even as late as 1792, when development was well advanced, as we saw earlier (chapter 4) a breach in the lower Liffey quay wall resulted in water reaching as far as Merrion Square, a distance of at least a mile. But where there's a will there's a way and fashion wanted to follow the earl – and it did. It took a while for the south side to displace the north side completely: like everything else, it was a process, not an event. As Whitelaw's census demonstrates, there was a rough equality of wealth on either side of the river just before the Act of Union (1801) – aye, and a rough equality of poverty too, as Whitelaw, as much as any contemporary, was to chronicle as a result of his many visitations to the homes of the Dublin poor. The scenes he described and the causes to which he ascribed the human wretchedness at the bottom of the Dublin heap required the reader to have a strong stomach: incredible overcrowding, with single rooms being subdivided into malodorous bed-spaces, not to mention the complete absence of any sanitation system – to be fair, a commonplace in all pre-modern cities. The result was stinking dung heaps, piled high with human and animal waste, in enclosed back yards. In some cases, he reported the resultant middens level with the first-floor windows of the houses. The condition of these dung heaps after heavy rain can be readily imagined, so please retain that strong stomach.

A sobering counterpoint to draw any account of Dublin's golden age towards a close.

Before that, let's take a short look at other south-side developments, not to the east but to the west of Grafton Street. Even before Carlisle Bridge established Grafton Street as the principal link southward, this area was advancing. South William Street had first been laid out as early as 1676, although its landmark building, Powerscourt House, was not completed until 1774. At the head of the street, where it meets Stephen Street, little more than a medieval lane at this time, Mercer's Hospital was established in 1734.

Another laneway, taking its name from its original function and its proximity to the castle, was Exchequer Street, which led directly on to a new street, Wicklow Street, thus completing the link back to Grafton Street. The other principal link street, named for the Earl of Chatham, dates from his time in power in the 1760s and completes the link west to the estate of Sir Francis Aungier around South Great George's Street, thus more or less filling in the area between Grafton Street and the environs of that street, which had existed as yet another medieval laneway until Aungier developed the area around it from 1685 onwards.

That was towards the west, but the more significant developments were to the east and disproportionately still north of the river. Here, the Gardiners expanded their holdings throughout the eighteenth century. Rocque's map of 1756 shows most of the area enclosed by Capel Street, Upper Dorset Street to North Frederick Street and east as far as Gardiner Street well filled in and Mountjoy Square already underway, although not fully completed until 1818. Plans for further western expansion, including a proposed oval circus at the western end of Eccles Street, were not realised. It was the first firm evidence of faltering purpose in the north-west quadrant.

Most of the lands thus developed belonged to the Gardiners. After a career garlanded with money and honours, Luke Gardiner the elder died in 1755. His sons, and most importantly his grandson Luke Gardiner the younger, who ascended to the peerage as viscount Mountjoy – thus the street and square names and also all the places named for Blessington, into which family the Gardiners had married – continued the patriarch's work.

The younger Luke Gardiner, Lord Mountjoy, was killed fighting for the crown forces against the Wexford rebels at the battle of New Ross on 5 June 1798, a reminder of where the primal loyalties of the creole ascendancy ultimately lay, despite their occasional political posturing. But it was those events – the insurrections in Wexford, east Ulster and, feebly and belatedly, County Mayo in 1798 – that brought the curtain down on the great age of the ascendancy, to be followed almost immediately by the Act of Union. Dublin did not stop developing, but the process slowed down; it gradually moved to the suburbs as the railway came along, but most of all it moved to the other side of the river and in particular to the south-east quadrant centred on Grafton Street and Leinster House.

It might have happened anyway but the opening of Carlisle Bridge in 1791 was a decisive accelerant, to put it at a minimum.

– ❀ –

EIGHT

THE HA'PENNY BRIDGE

I T'S NOT THE most obvious place for a bridge. O'Connell Bridge is just downstream and Capel Street Bridge just upstream. It's no great distance from the one to the other. Maybe not, but there was sufficient demand for a river crossing hereabouts that there was a ferry service, in the ownership of one William Walsh. It had been in operation for some time, but by the early nineteenth century, city inspectors deemed the ferries to be in a dangerous state. Walsh was told either to improve them or else see to the building of a bridge. He chose the bridge and agreed a toll charge of a ha'penny – a half a penny, the basic unit of imperial currency – for all who crossed it. It was to be a pedestrian bridge only, the first such in Dublin. For a while, the toll rose to a penny ha'penny, a three-times increase, before reverting.

Why the demand for any kind of crossing here, given the proximity of the other two bridges already noted? In a small way, this is one of the trickiest questions any historian must address, for the question itself is freighted with a mental image of the Liffey quays as they are in modern times. But they were quite different then, which helps to explain the demand for a crossing. Judging from contemporary prints, there was no segregation between pedestrian and vehicular traffic, specifically no raised pavements forbidden to carts and carriages.

And of these latter, there was no shortage. Nor were there disciplined traffic lanes, such as the modern city has, which try to keep some kind of segregated order between vehicles. The modern quays are, of necessity, one-way. In the early nineteenth century they were not. Carts, carriages, pedestrians – pretty much anything that moved – were jumbled together in an undisciplined two-way melee, with pedestrians the most obviously vulnerable category. This made the drag between the Capel Street and O'Connell Bridges hazardous, and it was in order to shorten that necessary journey to cross the river that the ferry service was established here.

It appears to have prospered. Walsh felt sufficiently confident in his market to assume the cost of erecting the bridge, with the toll – granted on a hundred-year lease – intended to recoup his capital costs and over time yield a profit for his enterprise. So it was. Walsh contracted a single-span metal bridge from the Coalbrookdale Company. Coalbrookdale was, and is, a village in the Ironbridge Gorge in Shropshire between Wolverhampton and Shrewsbury, close to the hideous modern town of Telford (was there ever a less deserved urban memorial to a great man?); it was an early centre of the industrial revolution.

Nearby is the village of Ironbridge, named for the bridge there thrown across the Severn, a sensation in its day, 1781. It was here that the technique whereby iron was smelted with coke was developed, making the production of iron a much cheaper process than hitherto. The Iron Bridge was the first such structure made of cast iron. It was a pioneering piece of pontine architecture, leading in its way to many later developments and improvements, of which the wonderful Clifton Suspension Bridge of 1864, further down the Severn at Bristol, is the most famous.

So, in the early years of the industrial revolution – which largely bypassed Dublin and most of Ireland – places like Coalbrookdale were where these new engineering skills in fashioning cast iron were concentrated. (It is somewhat ironic that just to its south is Wenlock Edge, one of the most ravishing rural landscapes in England and the subject for much of the poetry of A.E. Housman.) So Walsh knew where to look for his metal bridge. It was designed by John Windsor, one of the works foremen, and built at the Coalbrookdale Iron Works. Once the necessary safety certificates had been furnished to the Dublin Ballast Board, the local authority with responsibility for the river and the port, the work proceeded.

The bridge was to be a single span of 140 feet, about 42 to 43 metres, arched 11 feet (3.4 metres) above high water. It comprised three main ribs of cast iron set in stone abutments on either bank. Once the prefabricated pieces had been shipped from Shropshire to Dublin, they were set into the abutments, already in position, and the bridge opened on 20 May 1816.[1] Despite some grumbles from a minority – that a metal structure was inappropriate in a city that demanded stone bridges – the bridge was judged a triumph and a thing of beauty pretty much from the start.

It was named Wellington Bridge for the victor of Waterloo the previous year, a Dubbelin man, of course, not that Arthur was much in the way of acknowledging that. The name was colloquial, not official, and it never really stuck. Some objected to the informal naming, not considering Arthur 'the heart of the rowl',* which to

---

* A Dubellin expression, indicating a good sort or one of the best. The reference is to tobacco, which used to be landed at the docks in huge rolls. The outer tobacco, having been

be fair to him he wasn't. In time, it was called the Metal Bridge, then – more adhesively – the Ha'penny Bridge in a nod towards the toll. It's still known thus, although – in the maddening way of official renaming that runs like a sub-theme through this book – its official moniker is the Liffey Bridge.

The toll lasted for slightly more than a century, not being abandoned until 25 March 1919. A detachment of Irish Volunteers was posted from the GPO to the south side on Easter Monday 1916, at the beginning of the Easter Rising, and made its way across the Ha'penny Bridge where the toll keeper, in his booth on the southern side, demanded payment. He was invited to sling his hook – well, roughly that – and the lads proceeded on their way.

The bridge, when first built, connected Lower Liffey Street on the north side to the area known as the Bagnio Slip on the south. The slip was as it sounds, a slipway from which boats could be launched upon the river or dragged ashore. It appears to have been at the point where what is now Lower Fownes Street gives onto the river, which it did before Wellington Quay was fully embanked, a process not complete until about the same time as the bridge was built. So the actual Bagnio Slip – one of a number of such slipways hereabouts – had lain slightly downriver of the southern abutment of the bridge but sufficiently close to have given its name to the little area.

A bagnio was a wash house, from the Italian. But it was also code for a brothel, and there is general agreement that the wash house either doubled up as a brothel – not an unusual conjunction, whether in Dublin or anywhere else – or that a brothel operated nearby. As in all trading ports, with its comings and goings of

---

exposed to the elements, was dried up but the heart of the roll, not having been so exposed, retained its moist sweetness.

The Ha'Penny Bridge by Samuel Frederick Brocas, 1818

sailors and merchants, prostitution was commonplace. It is unsurprising, therefore, that there should have been a brothel in this district.

At around the same time as the bridge was built, there was also constructed Merchants Arch directly at the point where the bridge met the southern bank of the river. It is still there, a covered walkway giving direct access to Temple Bar Square. It was originally built as a guildhall, the last such ever erected in the city because the guild system was undone by the Municipal Corporations (Ireland) Act 1840 which, under the inevitable political influence of Daniel O'Connell, began the process of slowly democratising Irish local government. One of its direct consequences was that O'Connell was duly elected lord mayor of Dublin in 1841, the first Catholic to hold the office since the brief reign of the perfectly useless King James II (*Séamus a' chaca* or James the Shit), the last Catholic king of England, who showed preference for his co-religionists during his brief reign from 1685 to '91. So although the guild system was in serious decline and approaching death in 1822, when the Merchants Hall – to give it its official name, which never really stuck – was built as a place of assembly for the Guild of Merchants, built it was. It quickly assumed a more public commercial character, such as it still displays today.

Most of the discussion of the Liffey bridges in this book to date has focused on the contribution that each made to the development of the areas adjacent on both sides of the river. It is much harder to make out this case for the Ha'penny Bridge. Rather, it took advantage of some intense development and urban infill on both banks in the 150 or so years prior to its construction. Neither Liffey Street and environs nor the contemporary Temple Bar area amounted to much architecturally in 1816, but they were none the less crowded and busy. It made sense to facilitate a crossing point here, whether by ferry or by bridge.

In 1666, that is just 150 years before the erection of the Ha'penny Bridge, the lands either side of it were green fields. On the north side, the first reliable map after Speed is that of de Gomme and Phillips (1673), made just before the building of the four Ormond bridges. Church Street Bridge, still – although not now for long – is shown as the only crossing on the river. The area immediately to the north of where the bridge was built is shown by de Gomme and Philips as open land simply marked 'Abby Parkes', the caption running roughly along the line of today's Abbey Street, the historical reference being to the then long defunct St Mary's Abbey. The confluence of the Bradogue – a small north-side tributary long since culverted – and the Liffey is also shown.

On the south side, the land between Dame Street and the river is likewise shown as open fields, crossed from north to south by a laneway marked Dirty Lane,* running at right angles to a path already named 'Temple Lane' which gave onto open ground at the eastern end – roughly encompassing an area from the modern Aston Quay to Hawkins Street and in as far as the modern College Street, all simply marked as 'Ground taken in from the Sea'.

This reclaimed land was a consequence of the further extension of the Liffey quay walls eastward. As early as 1656, Sir John Temple, lawyer and politician, had been granted a lease on the open ground behind his house on Dame Street around what is now Fownes Street; the newly reclaimed land to the east enabled him to extend his property and establish the quarter that ever after bore his name, Temple Bar, running either side of the modern street bearing that name. But in the time of the de Gomme and Philips map, it was still undeveloped.

Not so by the time of Charles Brooking's map of 1728, just fifty years later. By then, the whole south shore of the Liffey, from Church Street Bridge east as far as the modern Hawkins Street, is solidly developed. The process continued and thickened thereafter, as can be clearly seen from Rocque's map (1756) and from the Ordnance Survey Six-Inch Map of 1837. This was northing (especially) and easting with a vengeance, a process that had begun in the 1680s with the erection of Bloody Bridge away upriver (chapter 3). Likewise on the north side, as with the growth of the Gardiner estate – and its minor tributary estates: Dominick, Archdall, Aldborough and others – up to Mountjoy Square and west to the line of Dorset Street.

---

* Dear old dirty Dubbelin was not short of Dirty Lanes. All or part of Bridgefoot Street was so named for a while, as was a ferry point on the north shore opposite Ringsend Point. There may well have been others; there was no shortage of dirt.

Less obvious on the north side was the process of infill that ran east from Capel Street to Sackville Street along the North Lotts, back as far as Abbey Street. The principal street in this artisanal area – dominated by warehouses, small workshops and such like – was Lower Liffey Street, connecting Abbey Street to the river. Through the middle of it, running parallel to Abbey Street and the river, was Strand Street. Because it is to this day an undramatic little quarter – Strand Street itself not much more than a glorified laneway – it is easily overlooked. But just like Temple Bar over the other side, it was a busy hive of commerce.

So instead of facilitating a process of development, the Ha'penny Bridge acknowledged one already present which gave it its *raison d'être*.

The Temple Bar area remained busy but suffered as much as anywhere in the general decline of Dublin in the course of the nineteenth century. Nor was the twentieth much kinder to it until its final decades, of which more later. The overall theme was one of neglect. Despite its location, plumb in the centre of the city between Dame Street – the principal commercial thoroughfare – and the river, no buildings of substance or ambition were built there. The whole place remained small-scale, unambitious, shabby.

Finally, in the second half of the twentieth century, the national transport company, Córas Iompair Éireann, gradually built up a property portfolio in the area. The intention was to build a central bus terminus. Inevitably, the entire process took time, and while plans were maturing buildings already purchased were leased at low rents on short-term leases. This attracted artists and small galleries and workshops and before long they began to define the area. Still, the larger transport plan remained on the table in the background, being regarded by its proposers as an urban *grand projet* that would be transformative. In this they were certainly correct, an insight that alarmed conservation groups as much as it excited the promoters.

Mercifully, a stop was put to this nonsense. The protesters – the usual ragbag of the discontented – captured the ear of Charles Haughey, by this time approaching the end of his scandal-ridden and corrupt time as Taoiseach. Haughey was a sad man, a supremely talented and intelligent politician but one who simply could not keep his sticky fingers out of the public till. In this, he had many opportunistic businessmen (they were indeed all men) to facilitate his avarice, with – of course – no favours asked for or received, the merest hint to the contrary instantly mobilising our learned friends in the Law Library. But he also affected to be a patron of the arts after the Renaissance fashion, without quite having the style to pull it off.

At any rate, he scuppered CIÉ's grand plan. In its place, he established a not-for-profit company, Temple Bar Properties, in 1991, primed with public funds. Its remit was to create anew a distinct cultural quarter for Dublin. We shall discuss its fortunes further in chapter 16.

The Ha'penny Bridge has, however, defied all attempts at change. There were advertisements in place along its sides for a time around the turn of the nineteenth century into the twentieth. That was deemed unseemly and unsightly – it was – and the ads were removed. The reason for the opposition to this defacement was that the bridge had long since been embraced in the popular imagination as the iconic structure in the city. It was the shape, even in rough outline, that came to stand for Dublin, rather as a squiggle of the billowing sail roofs of the

Sydney Opera House reminds you irresistibly of that building and that city and nowhere else.

From the start, artists were attracted to it as a subject. As early as 1817, Samuel Frederick Brocas (1792–1847) included his study of the bridge in his 'Select Views of Dublin'. Later, it lent itself particularly well to the shimmer of impressionism. Walter Osborne (1859–1903) was the most distinguished of the artists who were heavily influenced by impressionism and who depicted the bridge in that manner. He was followed by hosts of lesser artists, including Percy French – better known for his witty songs – and, in more modern times, photographers.

It is fitting. This modest but elegant single arched span seems about right for Dublin. We don't do grandiose.* We have no need of Eiffel Towers or Arcs de Triomphe or Empire State Buildings, having no achievements to justify such excess. The Liffey is a modest river and it has defined a modest city. The Ha'penny Bridge is an entirely appropriate and proportionate city icon.

However, this affection for the Ha'penny Bridge might not have saved it if W.B. Yeats had got his way. What happened was this. Hugh Lane (1875–1915), the nephew of Lady Gregory, had acquired one of the very finest collections of impressionist masterpieces in private hands in the British Isles. Lane had established himself as a successful fine-art dealer in London at an early age. In 1901, he visited an exhibition in Dublin of paintings by John Butler Yeats – the poet's father – and Nathaniel Hone (1831–1917).

---

* I can never hear that word without wishing to mispronounce it. Once, visiting the Stephansdom in central Vienna, I found myself behind a bored American tourist giving the impression that he was being dragged around Europe by his wife when he'd rather be knocking the little pill along the fourteenth fairway. He was unimpressed by the Dom. 'It's too grand-oyse,' quoth he, 'too grand-oyse.'

This sparked in Lane an interest in Irish art, to which he had hitherto been largely oblivious. He lent a significant part of his collection to the Dublin Municipal Gallery. Moreover, he offered the gallery the paintings as outright gifts on condition that an appropriate and permanent gallery be built to accommodate them. At the time, the Municipal Gallery was housed in temporary and unsatisfactory quarters in Harcourt Street.

Thus began the saga of the Lane pictures. A gallery was indeed designed, by none other than Sir Edward Lutyens, as part of a splendid stone bridge – very grand-oyse indeed – to replace the Ha'penny Bridge, which Lane described as 'the hideous metal bridge'. Yeats, in particular, whose word counted in artistic matters in Dublin, not least thanks to his own unceasing exertions, was delighted with Lutyens's proposed new bridge. However, the corporators of Dublin were not. The foundations would be too costly and what about the regular stink from the river beneath – the Liffey being more or less the *cloaca maxima* of the city at the time – and various other objections. These objections were trumpeted by newspapers in the ownership of William Martin Murphy (1844–1919), the most successful businessman of the day in Ireland.

Photograph of William Martin Murphy
from *Tramway & Railway World*, 1901

Murphy was a red rag to Yeats, a philistine bourgeois of the worst kind. But he bested Yeats, just as he bested Jim Larkin during the great lockout of 1913, the most famous labour dispute in Irish history. His objections to Lutyens's proposed bridge were the usual philistine hypocrisy that the money would be better spent on the poor and the sick. In fact, there appears to have been little stomach in official Dublin either for Lane or for his paintings or for Lutyens or for his bridge. Murphy was reflecting not just his own taste, or lack of it, but that of a public indifferent – if not actually hostile – to fine art. Yeats wanted 'monuments of our own magnificence', a brew far too heady for early twentieth-century Dublin.

Outraged by all this, Lane withdrew the offer and bequeathed his gift to the National Gallery in London. But in early 1915 – by now, he was director of the National Gallery of Ireland – he reversed his intention by adding a codicil to his will restoring the pictures to Dublin. Fatally, he did not witness the codicil and then drowned aboard the *Lusitania* when she was torpedoed by the German navy off the coast of his native County Cork.

The dispute over ownership of the Lane pictures rumbled on for most of the twentieth century; it was not until 1959 that an agreement was reached to share them alternately between London and Dublin. In the short-term, William Martin Murphy had won, and his victory announced the stupid philistinism of the newly independent Irish state, buttressed by its literary censorship and reactionary Catholicism. But Yeats had the victory of posterity.

Lutyens's bridge never got built. The Ha'penny Bridge remained in place, and there it stands today, Dublin's reticent, understated, elegant river arch.

– ❀ –

NINE

HEUSTON BRIDGE

UNTIL 1966, IT was simply King's Bridge. In 1922, in the renaming wave noted so many times previously in this text, it was changed to Sarsfield Bridge. But that name never stuck – funny how un-adhesive these new names could be. But at least most of them remained in place officially, even if the populace never adopted them in daily speech. But poor old Sarsfield never caught on at all, at any level. So King's Bridge it remained until 1966. Then Seán Heuston's name was adopted readily, as it was for the railway terminus adjacent. The 1916 connection was potent, especially in that golden anniversary year.

The bridge dates from 1828, and it defies the general thrust of this book. No northing and easting here. To the contrary, we are way upriver. At the time of its construction, it was the first bridge *below* Islandbridge and in quite the wrong direction relative to most of the bridges we have been reviewing thus far. So why is it here? Unlike most of the other bridges, it made no notable contribution to the development of the nearby districts and suburbs.

King's Bridge stood at the very western margin of the town at a time when developing Dublin was galloping off in the other direction, towards the bay. With the exception of the Liffey Viaduct (1877, see next chapter; and the James Joyce Bridge, chapter 17) it was the last crossing erected upstream of the cluster of Ormond bridges that dated from the 1670s and '80s. The Liffey Viaduct, as we shall see, was a direct consequence of the great railway terminus constructed nearby twenty years after the bridge. Otherwise, it wouldn't be there because there would be no requirement for it. As for the James Joyce gazebo, the less said the better, although it must be said later.

Various speculative schemes had, in fact, been mooted for a river crossing here from the early eighteenth century. The prompt was the building of the Royal Barracks (latterly Collins Barracks, now a campus of the National Museum of Ireland). The idea was to establish a secure route from the barracks to the Royal Hospital at the eastern margin of Kilmainham over on the south side. As we saw in chapter 2, this occupied a quite magnificent site along the top of the ridge that ran into town from Kilmainham as far as Christ Church, at the eastern end of what had been the lands of the Priory of the Knights Hospitallers of Jerusalem before the dissolution of the monasteries. It commanded – as it still does – a splendid view across the river to the Phoenix Park. It is the finest Caroline building in the city – indeed, almost the only building of real distinction put up in the seventeenth century. At the time of its construction, it was way out of town. By the time King's Bridge, as it became, was first mooted there had been much infill, and while it was still located well on the western margins, the expanding city was creeping towards it. Nearby, the very fine Dr Steevens's Hospital had been built in the 1720s and opened in

1733, with funds bequeathed by Dr Richard Steevens, an English medic who had settled in Dublin; it was designed by Thomas Burgh, he of the Royal Barracks and the Old Library in Trinity. It was something of a bonsai version of the Royal Hospital next door and was described by Maurice Craig as 'the last kick of the 17th century'.[1] In turn, next to it St Patrick's Hospital (Swift's Hospital, built with funds willed by the dean) opened in 1757, twelve years after the great man's death. Meanwhile, up the hill at Thomas Street, Arthur Guinness opened a brewery at St James's Gate in 1759, which did quite well afterwards. It was not all northing and easting in eighteenth-century Dublin, even though it was mostly so.

The Royal Hospital was primarily a retirement home for old soldiers. None the less, it was a military establishment and it was felt that some connection between the new Royal Barracks and the Royal Hospital was desirable. Dublin was then and after, until the end of British rule, a heavily militarised and garrisoned city. Knitting the military bits together was a priority. Shortly before the bridge was built, a military road was laid out that linked Bloody Bridge with the Royal Hospital.[2] (It was later extended and evolved into what we now know as St John's Road, but the line of the original military road can still be seen in a small turning off St John's Road that leads directly to the Royal Hospital.)

Now a fixed river crossing upstream of Bloody Bridge became a more urgent *desideratum*.

The proximate prompt for the bridge was the visit of King George IV in 1821. It was the first visit to Ireland by a British/ English monarch on a wholly peaceful mission in the 650 years since the insertion of the English crown into Irish affairs. The few of his predecessors who had been bothered to come to Ireland had

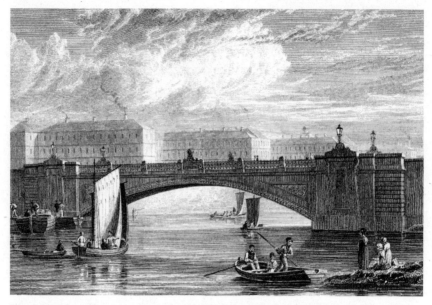

King's Bridge with the Royal Barracks in the background, 1832

done so purely out of occasional military necessity. But George IV came for no better reason than to spread balm among his Hibernian subjects. A public subscription raised £14,000[3] and this proved to be the seed money for the bridge. The king had expressed the wish that the bridge should be built. So it was, and so it was named.

It is not a thing of beauty, King's Bridge. It is narrow, less than 10 metres wide and 50 metres long. It is made of cast iron, slightly arched and has an anonymous, somewhat furtive appearance. It was hardly big enough for the early traffic it drew and certainly unsuitable for the volume of motorised traffic that was attracted once the internal combustion engine was invented. This led, in the fullness of time, to the building of the Frank Sherwin Bridge (see chapter 14) right beside it as a relief road crossing. These days, as well as pedestrians, it mainly carries the track of the Luas red line to and from the stop at Heuston Station.

Whether the original intentions behind the erection of the bridge were fulfilled, there is little doubt that the arrival of the railway was the making of it. It was one thing to provide an access link between two military establishments on either side of the river, but quite another thing suddenly to find on your doorstep the most revolutionary advance in human mobility since the Roman empire.

The railway, as we all know, first developed its potential for passenger and freight traffic in the United Kingdom. In the UK's western isle, the first railway was established in the south-east quadrant of the city, its urban terminus at Westland Row (now Pearse Station) close to the east end of Trinity College and around the corner from Merrion Square. The first train on this, the Dublin and Kingstown Railway, ran on 17 December 1834. It covered the roughly fourteen kilometres between Westland Row towards what is now Dún Laoghaire harbour in about twenty minutes.* This line is still extant and is the centrepiece of the Dublin Area Rapid Transit (DART) system, although since much extended north and south.

The Dublin and Kingstown Railway was critical in opening up the south-east suburbs of the city, hugging as it did the shores of Dublin Bay. It reinforced two trends already present. First, it confirmed the south-east as the key line of fashionable urban and suburban advance; second, it facilitated the flight of the well-to-do from the ever more decaying city centre towards the more salubrious surrounds of the bay. In time, various suburban stations and halts were studded along the route. For instance, it was at Sydney Parade

---

* That first train ran short of Kingstown, stopping at what is now Salthill & Monkstown, but the line was soon extended to Kingstown Harbour, by then the principal package port for the city, thus fulfilling the developers' original intentions.

station that Mrs Emily Sinico apparently committed suicide by throwing herself under a train in James Joyce's short story 'A Painful Case', one of the key texts in *Dubliners* (1914).

That was all at the eastern end of the city. At the western end, by King's Bridge, there emerged what turned out to be one of the two most ambitious railway development schemes in the country. This was the Great Southern & Western Railway (GS&WR), designed to build trunk routes to the principal cities of the south, Cork and Limerick. (The other big scheme, the Great Northern Railway, linked Dublin and Belfast with its Dublin terminus at Amiens Street, now Connolly Station, in the north-east quarter of the city.) A formidable issue of initial share capital in the GS&WR, to the tune of £1.3 million, was quickly snapped up by investors, as railway mania – one of the wonders of the age – began to bite in Ireland.

The first sod on this heroic enterprise was cut just west of Dublin in January 1845. A junction at Cherryville, County Kildare established a branch line to Carlow, which was completed and opened for business by August 1846. On the mainline, the route reached Maryborough (now Portlaoise) by June 1847. By March 1848, the line was as far south as Thurles, County Tipperary and then went on to Limerick Junction that July. By March 1849, it was into north County Cork at Mallow and finally, on 29 October that year, the GS&WR attained its temporary Cork terminus at Blackpool. (It took until 1855 to tunnel into the permanent terminus at Glanmire (now Kent) Station, hard by Penrose Quay on the Lee.) The distance completed was 160 miles (257 km). The line had been built, in the middle of the Great Famine, 'in its entirety in less than five years by a workforce that had no experience of railway construction'.[4]

There remained only the question of a Dublin terminus.

In the same year that the first sod was cut for the GS&WR, an advertisement in the *Freeman's Journal* solicited designs for a terminus. The site was chosen by Sir John Macneill, chief engineer of the railway company. It stood on the southern bank of the Liffey, a fraction upstream of King's Bridge. The act of 1844 incorporating the company decreed that 'the railway hereby authorised ... shall commence in a field at or near King's Bridge in the county of the city of Dublin between Military Road and the River Liffey',[5] which rather made Macneill's mind up for him. The winning entry, from over sixty received, was that of Sancton Wood, an English architect who had made railway design his speciality. He had already designed a number of early railway stations in London and nearby counties.

He did some further work in Ireland for the GS&WR, but Kingsbridge may with justice be considered his masterpiece. Maurice Craig describes it thus: 'a delightful building, a renaissance palazzo, gay* and full-blooded, with fruity swags and little domed towers on the wings, a thoroughgoing formal composition, excellently articulated'.[6] The work was executed in local stone by Dublin contractors and the coats of arms of the three cities the railway was to serve – Dublin, Cork and Limerick – were displayed on the splendid east front of the station building, looking along the quays towards the city centre.

There were, of course, problems. The route of the railway impinged on lands belonging, on the one side, to the Royal Hospital and, on the other, to the military at a barracks near Islandbridge. There were the usual rows and wrangles but the

---

* Craig was writing in the early 1950s, before the word had acquired the common currency of its present-day meaning.

Kingsbridge Terminus (latterly Heuston Station), c. 1880–1900

railway was *the* irresistible technology of the age – and so it was barrelled through.

The station itself has been much modernised over the years and new platforms added, up to a total number of ten. It remains the principal railway terminus for the city, having double the number of mainline platforms as its nearest rival, Connolly Station in Amiens Street. During the 1916 Rising, it proved a vital lifeline to British troops sent up from the Curragh Camp, about fifty-five kilometres away in County Kildare – and directly on the line of the GS&WR – to garrison the city in revolt. It had originally been part of the rebels' plans to occupy Kingsbridge Station, but the Rising – planned in secret by a tiny cabal of radicals – went off at half-cock when the formal leadership of the Irish Volunteers got word of it at the last minute and countermanded all mobilisation orders. The result was that the numbers actually turning out on Easter Monday 1916 were way below original expectations, meaning that the plan to invade Kingsbridge Station had to be abandoned. That left the way clear for the British relief troops coming up from the Curragh to detrain there unopposed. It was a similar story at Amiens Street Station, the Great Northern Railway terminus.

By then, 1916, the great Victorian railway system stood at its apogee before the wholesale triumph of the internal combustion engine. Road transport was only then in its infancy, although soon to show its muscle; the railway had helped to create a national retail economy by delivering goods at previously unimaginable speeds to the provinces, including many remote parts thereof. The fact that many of the branch lines built for this distributive purpose were never remotely capable of paying their way or recovering their development costs – let alone turning a steady profit – was less of an inhibition than it might seem. Once the national retail and distribution system had been called into existence, it was a beast that required feeding. The price only became a debilitating factor once lorries and cars and roads established their primacy after 1918. Then the railways began their long decline, in Ireland as elsewhere.

But in its pomp, Kingsbridge Station had a fair claim to be the umbilicus of the entire national system. What was beyond dispute was its pre-eminence as the finest piece of railway architecture in Ireland. Without it, it is hard to imagine that the Liffey bridge adjacent would have amounted to as much as it did for as long as it did.

In the great renaming of 1966, it became Heuston Station. Seán Heuston (1891–1916) had gained employment as a clerk with the GS&WR and was posted to Limerick. A convinced republican from an early age, he formed one of the country's largest branches of the Fianna – a republican youth group that became a recruiting and training ground for members of the Irish Volunteers and later of the IRA. He turned out for the Rising on Easter Monday 1916 and was put in charge of a sub-garrison at the Mendicity Institute on Usher's Island, just up along the southern quays from the station. The idea was to harass those British reinforcements which had come up from the Curragh, had detrained at Kingsbridge and were marching along the quays to their allotted positions.

He succeeded beyond anyone's expectations. He maintained his position for forty-eight hours, his tiny group taking advantage of the firing positions afforded by the rising ground to the rear of their position. Heuston's men accounted for over a hundred British casualties before they were eventually overrun. It was an unexpectedly impressive performance by amateur volunteers led by what was little more than a young fellow. Certainly, James Connolly – the commander-in-chief of the rebels – never envisaged the little position, outnumbered ten to one, holding out that long or inflicting anything like the damage it did. He mainly thought of it as a harassing nuisance offering some cover to the more substantial Volunteer position at the Four Courts across the river. Accordingly, it had been starved of rations and ammunition, which made its achievements even more impressive.

Understandably, the British were utterly enraged by the success of this paltry group and they determined to root them out. They surrounded Heuston's position at the rear, preventing any escape up the hill from where Heuston and his men might have re-joined one of the other Volunteer garrisons at the South Dublin Union. The final British assault came at noon on the Wednesday and lasted about an hour. A couple of British troops were able, with real courage, to get to the windows of the Mendicity and lob in some bombs. That did it. Within the hour, Heuston had shown the white flag; his little position was the first rebel redoubt to surrender. He was executed in Kilmainham Gaol on 8 May, almost two weeks after the surrender. At twenty-five, he was the youngest of the 1916 leaders to be shot.

As to the bridge, it was quite overshadowed by the station. Without the station, this would have remained a rather sleepy part of town, remote from all the evolving excitements of the northing and easting towards the bay. But with the station, it was a constant hive of humanity. Even with the relative decline of the railways in the course of the twentieth century, the bridge provided sufficient capacity for the motorised traffic that met people off the trains. Ireland remained a poor country for most of the twentieth century, with correspondingly low levels of private car ownership by international standards.

Once that improved, the number of cars rose – it was a key indicator of consumer desire and private prosperity – and the sheer volume of traffic proved too much for dear old King's Bridge. Renamed Heuston Bridge, along with the station, it was finally bypassed in 1982 by the erection of Frank Sherwin Bridge, as we have already noted and will see again in chapter 14.

It stood largely idle, a rather forlorn and neglected orphan, until redeployed as part of the Luas red-line tram route in 2004. That is its principal function today: just beside it is the Heuston Luas stop to serve the station. It is constantly busy, for it links the station to the city centre and to Connolly, the other principal mainline station. So once again, as almost from the start of its life, the purpose of the bridge is determined almost entirely by the station and by the requirement to get passengers to and from it. The original intention that prompted the building of the bridge, to link the Royal Barracks and the Royal Hospital, seems almost comically anachronistic now. That's the way things go. Stuff happens, circumstances change, revolutionary technology is transformative. It kills some things stone dead, just as the railway killed the canals and the car killed the pony and trap.

But it is harder to kill off a bridge. It is awfully permanent, even if standing there idle and bereft of function as Heuston Bridge was for more than twenty years. The city might have knocked it down, as now surplus to requirements, but that probably seemed more trouble than it was worth. Then, hallelujah!, along came the fancy new trams – continental style – to give the old girl a new lease of life.

– ❦ –

TEN

LIFFEY VIADUCT

THIS IS THE bridge that nobody sees. It has never been renamed so is not subject to the same confusion that dogs other Dublin bridges – it is simply unknown to most people. From the name, it seems to cross the Liffey somewhere, but where? It could be away out in County Kildare or otherwise beyond the western boundaries of the city for all that people might guess.

But it's in town all right, well upriver to be sure, between King's/Heuston Bridge and Islandbridge. It's not at all invisible, but it is not easily seen because it runs considerably below street level. A pedestrian would have a reasonable chance of spotting it, looking down while walking along the south side of Conyngham Road if not otherwise preoccupied, but a motorist – much more likely to be found on that thoroughfare – would miss it entirely. The best view of all is from the apartments built just south of the river on the site of the abandoned Clancy Barracks at the end of the South Circular Road.

Conyngham Road stands well above the marshalling yards

and outer platforms of Heuston Station. They lie immediately to the south of it, and the Liffey Viaduct would not be there – there would be no need for it – were it not for the station. Nor would there be any need for it if the development of the Irish railway system in the nineteenth century had followed a more rational plan of development.

It didn't. Unsurprisingly, as part of the United Kingdom, it followed British political culture in addressing this revolutionary technology. British commercial culture, and English common law in particular with its very tight protections for property and the security of commercial contracts, discouraged direct state involvement in large infrastructural schemes – and in the 1830s and '40s, there was nothing bigger, or even close to, the railways in terms of infrastructure. The British were happy to leave the process to private initiative, with the state only endorsing developments by act of parliament. Even then, members voting for this proposal or that were generally not concerned with the overall strategic development of an integrated national system but rather whether the proposed line might affect their constituencies for good or ill. Additionally, there was the question of whether individual members might have a personal financial interest in the development proposal.

The continental experience was quite different, reflecting a different political culture. Most continental countries were more top-down and *dirigiste* in their commercial thinking than Britain. While this certainly had the effect of discounting such public opinion as was available, it had the advantage of planned strategic thinking, which avoided much of the chaotic duplication of effort that was the product of sundry private initiatives under the British system. The first country on the continent to develop its railway system was Belgium. To this day, the Belgian railway system – the densest in the world per square kilometre – has at its centre the two great crossed mainlines. One runs north–south from Antwerp through Brussels and Namur to Liège and Arlon, next door to Luxembourg, in the south. The other is west to east, from Ostend through Brussels to Liège and on towards Aachen and Germany. From these two cruciform mainlines, the rest of the Belgian system is projected.

This strategic planning reflected the influence of French political culture with its emphasis on centralised, rational administration rather than the clamour of representative and potentially fractious institutions like the House of Commons. It affected all neighbouring countries, not least Germany – still to be unified in a single state – where the railways laid out in small individual states were generally not extensive enough to yield a commercial return unless co-ordinated with those in bordering states. For example, the line from Leipzig to Dresden in Saxony was extended to Magdeburg in neighbouring Brandenburg, now Saxony-Anhalt, and proved a great success. The development of a national German railway system *prior to* the political unification of the country facilitated that very political union.[1]

The British system had none of this coherence. It was based on private initiatives resulting in furious competition and the inevitable duplication of effort that this entailed, as different companies pursued the most likely and promising routes. Thus the necklace of four mainline stations, all within walking distance of each other, along the Marylebone Road in London – Marylebone, Euston, St Pancras and King's Cross – each a terminus for a company offering services to and from the north.

As London went, Dublin followed. By the end of the 1860s,

there were no fewer than five mainline termini for the small city, with no connection between them: Kingsbridge for the GS&WR; Broadstone for the Midland Great Western; Amiens Street (now Connolly) for the Great Northern Railway; Westland Row (now Pearse) for the Dublin South-Eastern; and Harcourt Street for the suburban commuter line, a branch of the Dublin South-Eastern, that ran inland through the southern suburbs to Bray.

The problem was to join them up. Which is where the Liffey Junction comes in. It was the first practical attempt to do so. There were, over time, a number of utopian proposals for a sort of Dublin *hauptbahnhof* that would integrate the lot, but they were never feasible and none got farther than the drawing boards of idealistic planners. (Even Paris, with its culture of rational administration, never managed this, thus the six mainline termini in the city centre to this day.) The answer was to try to link them. That necessitated the extension of existing lines to meet up with others, which is what the Liffey Viaduct was for.

It meant tunnelling under the Phoenix Park. But first, the river had to be crossed. This was done between 1872 and 1877. The Liffey Viaduct is similar in design to the much larger Loopline Bridge (chapter 12), also known officially as the Liffey Viaduct although it is never so-called, meaning that the name is reserved for this bridge alone. It is reminiscent of the Loopline in its appearance, comprising the triangular wrought-iron latticework typical of many late-Victorian railway bridges. It was a system first developed in Great Britain and brought to Ireland by Sir John Macneill of the GS&WR, whom we have already met as chief engineer to that company. He had previously worked in England for ten years with the great civil engineer Thomas Telford, who was probably the principal developer of this triangular system.

Terminus of the Midland Great Western Railway at Broadstone Station, c. 1860

This Liffey Viaduct is altogether neater as well as more discreet than the Loopline. It manages to be both functional and elegant. Once over the Liffey, the new line that it carries disappears into a tunnel, 692 metres long – the longest railway tunnel in the city – that carries it under the Phoenix Park. It runs just west of the Wellington Monument and under Chesterfield Avenue to emerge again in a cutting just north of the North Circular Road gate of the park. From there it runs up to Glasnevin Junction, where it joins the Midland Great Western's Liffey branch. The Midland, whose passenger terminus was nearby at Broadstone, had been the first railway company to open a branch that gave them access to the valuable goods trade in Dublin Port. As with so much in the city's history, the gaze towards the sea and seaborne trade represented a magnetic draw for all urban development.

The GS&WR had the disadvantage of possessing the most westerly of all Dublin's railway termini. It was absolutely at the wrong end of the city, yet it understandably wished to get access to the port. Thus the bridge and the tunnel. On the way up to Glasnevin Junction, there was a halt on the line near the recently opened cattle market, at the top of Prussia Street by the North Circular Road, where beasts for export could be loaded aboard. From Glasnevin the line followed the line of the Royal Canal – also owned by the Midland Great Western Railway – to the Church Road Junction at East Wall. Along the way, it ran at the back of the northern end of what later became Croke Park, the largest sports stadium in Ireland, for which that end – the railway end – was named. (That end also holds the fabled Hill 16.) From Church Road Junction the Midland line went on to the Midland Yard, about halfway along the North Wall, while the GS&WR's line branched off to a goods terminal of its own at the junction of East Wall Road and the end of the North Wall. This yard was known to old railway men as the Southern Point. (This was confusing, as it stood downriver to the east; but the southern reference nodded to its owners, the GS&WR.) When the yard became redundant in the second half of the twentieth century, it was reconfigured as a large concert venue and the name partially retained as simply the Point, which opened in 1989. Today it is the 3Arena.[2]

This seems as good a moment as any other to consider two processes, laboriously but persistently carried through over time, without which Dublin would not be the city it is. They are the embanking of the river and the reclamation of land from the sea, the city's eternal friend and enemy.

The embanking of the river, while straightening its course in the process, was a piecemeal process of centuries. It was often undertaken under licence by new riverside landowners like Jervis and Ellis to enhance their own holdings, while also prompting the building of new bridges to access the new quays thus developed. The two processes were related. It is easy for the modern Dubliner to forget just how unruly and all over the place the unimpeded flow of the river was. So lost is it to memory, so accustomed are we to the discipline wrought by the quays, that we must rely on scholarly reconstructions in cartographic form of the Liffey's natural course.

Such reconstructions rely on inference and on the few existing maps we have of the un-embanked river, of which Speed's map (1610) is the most suggestive.* Prior to Speed, all is inference, albeit well-informed – it's not mere guesswork. But Speed gives us a glimpse, if little more, of the untrammelled course of the river. Upriver of Church Street Bridge – then the only river crossing in the city – there is nothing on either bank to impede the natural course of the waterway. Downriver of Church Street are the earliest quays below the medieval town, with Wood Key [*sic*] and Marchants Key [*sic*] clearly identified but no others. These earliest quayside developments were unsurprisingly located there and were designed to enable simple commerce, the loading and unloading of merchandise.

What is quite startling to the modern eye – accustomed to the disciplined containment of the river all the way down to the docks – is the sudden billow on the south bank immediately to the east of the medieval core. The Poddle, not yet culverted, joins the main river here, whose natural tidal flow inundates what are now Wellington Quay and Aston Quay. On the north bank, Speed

---

* It is worth recording that, as far as is known, Speed never actually visited Dublin and relied on surveys conducted by others, most likely Sir John Davies, the attorney-general in the Dublin Castle administration.

shows sundry little tributary confluences, that of the Bradogue in particular. Reconstructions speculate that the riverbank in its natural state occupied much of what is now Lower O'Connell Street. So it continued downriver.

Barely a hundred years later, Charles Brooking's map (1728) shows all this being transformed. The quays are now well developed – not continuously: there are still a few gaps, as at Wellington Quay, still in development in Brooking's time, although shown complete by Rocque (1756) less than thirty years later. What is shown as early as Brooking's map, however, is the sheer extent of the embanking, all the way along to Sir John Rogerson's Quay on the south bank, with the development of the North Wall on the other side already in train. Brooking's map already shows the trammelled course of the Liffey due to its progressive embankment. It looks like the modern city, quite unlike the undisciplined watercourse that had flowed for the nine centuries or so prior to Brooking.

As with the development of the quays, so went the other taming of the old enemy: the reclamation of land from the sea. The point at which the North Wall ends – the Point – is where it meets East Wall Road, curving around from Annesley Bridge over the Tolka. These two roads, plus roughly the North Strand to the west, denominate the area known as East Wall. It is all reclaimed land, a process begun in the eighteenth century. We can recall Lord Aldborough (chapter 4) enjoying the marine view from his big town house at what is now the Five Lamps, with the area to the east still undeveloped. But it was developed, first into 132 lots of land which were to be protected from tidal inundations. This was done gradually, thus spoiling Aldborough's view. In the process, from about the 1820s onwards, the area thus contained developed its own personality, becoming a snug working-class suburb supplying labour to the expanding docks adjacent.

It is hardly an accident that the road containing the East Wall district on its west side was the North Strand Road. It is still there, the principal access route from the north-eastern suburbs to the city centre. But prior to the land reclamations of the eighteenth and nineteenth centuries, it was the shoreline, thus the name. These developments, together with the canalising of the lower Tolka (echoing the Liffey quays in miniature) and the reclamation of all of what is now Fairview and its eponymous park, remained a work in progress not completed until the early twentieth century. As late as 1907, the embankment carrying the Belfast railway at Clontarf is still shown running over open water, Fairview Park not yet having been reclaimed from the sea.[3] So the entire process was the work of centuries. The Clontarf shoreline, although on the tidal estuaries of both the Liffey and the Tolka, had reclaimed enough land in the middle ages to leave it above sea level at high water, thus facilitating the early establishment of its castle and of the curing sheds for herrings at what is now the end of Vernon Avenue (a name memorialised in the name of a well-known pub, the Sheds).

On the south shore, the building of the Great South Wall facilitated the reclamation of dry land from the sea in its lee. Although not as dramatic or extensive a process of reclamation as that on the north side, it was impressive none the less. The undisturbed shoreline had run, it appears, from Merrion Gates back towards town at a pub in Irishtown known as the Conniving House, where the modern junction of Beach Road and Marine Drive now is.[4] To the seaward of this line lay all of what would in time become Sandymount. As late as 1834, the earliest image we have of the brand-new Dublin and Kingstown Railway shows its embankment at Booterstown, with its landward side – now a charming nature reserve – still subject to tidal inundation.

This did indeed contrast with the north shore. In Clontarf, there is cartographical evidence of a possible defined coastal track as early as late medieval times – indicating some kind of embanking protection against tidal inundation – and solid evidence of a roadway from the late seventeenth century on.[5] On the south shore, however, things happened later. Everything between Ballsbridge (Merrion Road) and the sea was only gradually reclaimed. Terra firma extended south from Ringsend only as far as the Conniving House. From there, all the modern Strand Road to the Merrion Gates was still shingle; behind it, towards Ballsbridge, was marshy ground still subject to the tide at high water. There appears to have been a lough of some sort where Park Avenue now stands. The earliest date for any kind of housing on what is now Park Avenue is about 1820.[6]

But after that things moved quickly. A Martello tower was built on the foreshore between 1804 and 1806, at the height of fears of an invasion by the French. It stood alone until the coast road reached it later in the century. There had been brickworks hereabouts in the eighteenth century. Gradually, the area began to fill in, dry above high water. Foundation dates are telling: St John's Church of Ireland church, at the junction of St John's Road and Park Avenue, dates from 1850; the nearby Star of the Sea Roman Catholic church from 1853; Presbyterian and Methodist churches were added in the second half of the nineteenth century. By 1865, the process was sufficiently advanced for Sandymount Avenue, running from Sandymount Green – itself already reclaimed ground and first laid out in the early nineteenth century – west towards Ballsbridge to be the birthplace of W.B. Yeats in what was by then a settled area. So the area had quickly established itself over the previous fifty to sixty years.

It appears that the original natural shoreline had run south from Ringsend along what is now roughly the line of Tritonville Road, so that the entire reclamation area was quite extensive. By the second half of the nineteenth century, Sandymount is solidly established: its three cricket clubs give the establishment dates of their present grounds as 1868 for Pembroke, just to the west of Park Avenue; 1904 for Railway Union, on the seaward side of Park Avenue; and 1911 for YMCA, a short distance away at the western end of Claremont Road. Newbridge Avenue, nearby and leading towards Ballsbridge, dates from the 1830s.

Then there was the railway, the Dublin and Kingstown, dating from the same decade. It ran through these reclaimed lands without any need for embanking or other artificial requirement, as at Booterstown farther out, still subject to the highest tides until finally embanked later.

All of which has carried us a very long way from the Liffey Viaduct. But the viaduct was a railway bridge pure and simple, and the effect of the railway was not only to destroy distance relative to historical precedent, but also to project change and development far from its ostensible source. It is hardly possible to imagine two points in Dublin more distant one from the other than Islandbridge and Merrion Gates. Yet the railway, and the land reclamation that it further encouraged, has established a definite connection between them. In the 1870s, no other technology in history could even have conceived of such a connection. None the less, there it is.

– ❀ –

ELEVEN

BUTT BRIDGE

Y<small>OU MIGHT HAVE</small> thought that with the construction of Carlisle Bridge, and its later widening to its present more-or-less rectangular shape, the process of easting was as complete as contemporary demands dictated. On terra firma, that perhaps held true, with this bridge's decisive effect on the urban street pattern and the creation of the processional route noted in chapter 7. But on the river, it was not so. We have seen that the long-desired widening was finally accomplished in 1880. Yet within a mere ten years, it was deemed not good enough and a further push to the east – yes, east again, the relentless pattern – was deemed necessary.

In fact, as far back as 1837, long before the widening of O'Connell Bridge, the agitation had begun for yet another bridge downriver. The pressure came from a group of Dublin merchants and was sustained over the coming decades. As the reader will have discerned by now, none of the infrastructural developments in the city that we now take utterly for granted, as if they were timeless artefacts of fate, were built without dispute, prevarication and delay. As many as may have wanted them, there were as many again who were opposed – and often in a position to obstruct.

The agitation was sustained. In 1852, a new committee was established by the merchants to urge upon the Port and Docks Board, the statutory body responsible, the need to build another downriver bridge. The chairman of this committee was the Earl of Charlemont, no less. The board disagreed, opting instead for the widening of Carlisle Bridge. In some respects, this widening was intended as a kind of sop, to deflect and mollify the merchants' agitation. The difficulties were deemed, in the board's opinion, to be insurmountable. What these difficulties were was not specified by the board, but given that the bridge was actually built less than thirty years later, they can't have been *that* insurmountable.[1]

The centrality of the Port and Docks Board in all this was a product of the fact that Dublin was first and last a trading port before it was any kind of a city. As it grew, it became two entities in one, neither one stronger than the other and each dependent on the other. Each required separate management. In the early days of the Normans, the control of the Liffey's tidal waters was vested in the crown: anyone holding property upon its banks had no jurisdictional influence. But with the expansion of trade in the sixteenth century, that changed and certain responsibilities were devolved upon riverine property holders, with crown grants giving long-term leases to individuals in return for the maintenance of quay walls and other essential infrastructure. In 1707, a Ballast Office was built and legislation passed to create a body to superintend its functions, and those of the port in general.[2]

This Ballast Board is the lineal ancestor of the various authorities which have overseen the governance of the port. It was originally a sub-unit of the corporation, but in time – given

the centrality of marine commerce to the fortunes of the city and
the contiguity of the port – it developed into a separate authority.
By 1869, a Dublin Port and Docks Act made its way through
parliament, defining the jurisdiction of the authority:

> Dublin Harbour is any space between Carlisle Bridge
> and the space one mile east of the Poolbeg Lighthouse in
> which a ship can lie and obtain shelter or unship goods
> or passengers.
> Dublin Port consists of the River Liffey and the quays and
> walls bounding it including the north, south and east walls,
> together with the bridges, piers, jetties and tidal basins
> belonging [*sic*] to the board and the strands, bays and
> creeks between Barrack Bridge, the harbour of Sutton on
> the north side and the harbour of Dalkey on the south but
> excluding Kingstown harbour and the Royal Canal Docks.

Which is why the merchants' committee, Charlemont and all,
in the 1850s was urging the building of a new bridge upon the
board, the board being the statutory and appropriate authority to
adjudicate upon the matter. That they answered the merchants in
the negative turned out to be neither here nor there; the widening
of Carlisle Bridge made sense on its own terms but did not obviate
the requirement for something in addition. The merchants were
not merely being stubborn. They had a point. Something more
was required downriver.

They got their way in the end. There was indeed a need
for another bridge, which was acknowledged in the legislation
authorising the widening of Carlisle Bridge. It was, however, to
be a swivel bridge with a central opening to allow ships upriver
to berth at Eden Quay and Burgh Quay. Anyone familiar with

photographs of late Victorian Dublin will recall the cluster of such ships right up to Carlisle Bridge, beyond which, of course, they could no longer go. It was barely two hundred years since the erection of Capel Street Bridge; in that time, the whole centre of gravity of the city had pushed east, away from the medieval core below Christ Church. That was impressive for a place that had had a continuous existence since Viking times with very little urban development to show for the period antecedent.

That is the background and context in which Butt Bridge came into existence. It is a useful reminder of the centrality of the river and of the commercial life that was the entire purpose of its settlement from antiquity and which by extension sustained the city itself. All this despite the evident difficulties that historical Dublin Bay had presented for shipping, with its great gaping maw inviting traffic but then frustrating it with silting and sandbars and other navigational hazards, which account for all the relief harbours dotted north and south, as noted in the definitional 1869 legislation.

One might wonder at this stage what the merchants had been on about for all those years. Basically, it boiled down to traffic movement on the streets. The easting process pushed the north–south axis in that direction. The bridge was needed to ease the congestion that had built up around Sackville Street. A survey in 1860 showed that 1,037 vehicles passed over the unwidened Carlisle Bridge each hour – almost as many as crossed London Bridge: 1,091.[3] That alone might have made the case for widening Carlisle Bridge *and* constructing another one downstream. The merchants had more than a point, and in the end they got their way on both scores. Butt Bridge provided a new river crossing to ease the pressure. It had the added merit of making road access between the fast-developing inner suburbs either side of the river

'We Serve Neither King nor Kaiser' – Irish Citizen Army lined up under a banner outside Liberty Hall, 1914

– Clontarf and Sandymount, for instance – easier.

As to the bridge itself, it was constructed to the design of the port engineer, Bindon Blood Stoney, a remarkable man of whom we shall hear more presently. He was also, as we have seen, involved in designing the widened Carlisle Bridge a little upriver. His name is included on the commemorative plaque which can still be seen on that bridge.

The new bridge was a simple, elegant design, in no way showy, and low-slung. It was a four-span bridge, with masonry arches projecting from the quaysides and with a central pier set into the riverbed. This pier supported the swivels: in two parts, they each rotated horizontally, allowing a navigation channel of 12 metres on either side, so that shipping had ingress to and egress from the upper quays. It was known initially as the swivel bridge.

It was soon renamed for the recently deceased Isaac Butt. A barrister and politician, he was one of those who had the dubious honour of being included in a book entitled *Worsted in the Game*, with the rather harsh subtitle of 'Losers in Irish History', being a series of essays about nearly men and women in Irish history – people who might have won gold but had to settle for silver at best and were lucky to be in the medals at all.

Butt was an Irish nationalist Tory, a species almost unimaginable today. But in his day – his day being roughly the decades after the Famine – allegiances were very fluid. It took the genius of Butt's nemesis, Parnell, to solidify them in a manner that we recognise. He was a Protestant, but an Irish Protestant, and although his own politics, despite softening over time, were always remote from those of the Fenians, he none the less defended Fenian prisoners in court with some skill and never doubted the sincerity of their convictions. He was the founder of the Irish home-rule tradition, setting up a body which went through a number of name changes but always retained at its heart those magic two words: 'home rule', brilliantly ambiguous. You could make of those words a number of things – as things quickly transpired, people did – but at their heart was a demand for autonomy from London in domestic Irish matters. Butt's parliamentary leadership of his group was rather too gentlemanly for some of his more robust colleagues, of whom Parnell was foremost. He was ousted from the leadership in 1877, to be replaced by the same Parnell, and died a couple of years later without quite reaching his sixty-fifth birthday.

It was all sufficient, however, to gain him a place in the Irish nationalist pantheon, albeit a couple of rungs down from the likes of Parnell and, later, the 1916 martyrs. Back in 1879, with him only just dead and the memory of him still fresh in the public consciousness, it seemed appropriate to call the new swivel bridge after him. And, mercy of mercies, because he was of the pantheon the bridge was not renamed for some other worthy at independence, thus saving us from further nomenclatural confusion, as if there wasn't enough along the Liffey bridges already.

The main point of Butt Bridge was to facilitate road traffic and create a new crosstown corridor. But it was narrow and it did not take long for complaints to issue and for an agitation to widen it to be heard. The opening swivel proved to be handy but inadequate, especially as larger commercial shipping, developing all the time, found berthages at Eden Quay and Burgh Quay less and less desirable. This was partly a product of the impressive contemporary development and expansion of the downriver port, with its deeper berthages and growing infrastructure.

Like a stuck record or something on an audio loop, the agitation to widen the bridge reprised an old Dublin theme: prevarication from the city authorities. It took twenty years of negotiating, admittedly with a political revolution interposing, before the matter was settled in 1932. It was finally agreed that closing the swivel – by now effectively redundant anyway – was in order and that the bridge was to be widened. There was an interesting caveat: that another bridge for traffic relief be built further downriver at Guild Street as a *quid pro quo*, something that never happened.

At any rate, Butt Bridge was redesigned, widened to 19 metres and opened in 1932. With the swivel gone, it was down from four to three spans and was the first bridge on the Liffey to be constructed with reinforced concrete. It meant that the river upstream was now closed to shipping and could accommodate barges only through the bridges' narrow eyes, and then only when tidal conditions provided sufficient draught. So once more, things moved east, downriver.

The logic of the traffic corridor across the bridge depended very much on the streets both adjacent and giving direct access to it. The north side had been stable for a long time, since Beresford Place had been there since the eighteenth century. A version of it can be seen as early as Rocque's map of 1756, where it is shown as an extension of Abby [*sic*] Street leading to The Strand – that is, the modern Amiens Street. But it is marked on the Ordnance Survey map of 1837 and shown in all its curvilinear elegance wrapping around the back of the Custom House, which was of course not yet there in Rocque's day.

The south side was slower to catch up. The building of the old Carlisle Bridge in the 1790s cut off Aston Quay to the south, leaving nothing on the north bank to connect with George's Quay downstream. The ubiquitous Wide Streets Commissioners were soon on the case. They had one major problem, namely that a brewery, owned by one William Sweetman, stood astride the proposed route. It occupied an area between the Carlisle Bridge and what is now Tara Street; worse, it extended right to the river's edge.

Sweetman saved the day in 1810 by offering part of his property to facilitate the progress of the new quay. Naturally, he wanted compo for his generosity, and just as naturally, the Ballast Board thought that he wanted too much. As Eamon Kelly used to say: 'things rested so', at least until 1816 when agreement was finally reached and the quay was completed. Mind you, Sweetman must have felt some pressure, because the commissioners had gone ahead with the rest of the project anyway, and were otherwise well advanced when the matter was finally settled.

The quay was named for Elizabeth Burgh, the first wife of Anthony Foster, one of the ascendancy grandees who had graced the old Irish parliament before it committed hara-kiri in 1800 and effected the Act of Union with Britain. Elizabeth had died a long time before, in 1744, so the naming was an act of posthumous uxorious piety. Her son, John Foster, was the last speaker of the old House of Commons.[4]

Tara Street was gradually patched together over time, not being complete in its modern form until after the erection of the original Butt Bridge, which seems to have acted as a stimulus to its consolidation. A version of it is shown as early as Brooking's map (1728) and marked as George's Street, giving on to the river at George's Quay adjacent. By the time of the Ordnance Survey map of 1837, it was shown in two parts, one still called George's Street (to Poolbeg Street) and the rest marked as Shoe Lane. By the mid-century, the whole street was dilapidated and let in tenements.[5] It did not become Tara Street until the first decade of the twentieth century, assuming its full modern course and having been improved.

It's another example, if one were needed, of the direct effect the major bridges had on their immediate surroundings. It may well have been that Tara Street would have developed more or less as it did anyway, but the presence of the new bridge was – to put it at its least estimation – a considerable incentive to join the dots by improving its condition, since it gave direct access to the bridge from the south side.

Butt Bridge was the last bridge over the river to be built for about a hundred years if you don't include the wretched Loopline railway viaduct, which, out of a sense of duty and dreary consistency, we must address next. Let's put that in some perspective. Dublin was founded sometime in the ninth century. For eight hundred years, it had only one bridge in the urban core – and then not for all of that time. Then, in barely two hundred years it added another eight, nine if you include the Liffey Viaduct. At which point, the bridge-building frenzy stopped, and it seems to me that it stopped for a good, or at least plausible, reason.

Butt Bridge was effectively the eastern limit of the town. To which you might object, what about the downriver docks? That's the point. The docks, all east and downriver of Butt Bridge, between it and the open sea, were becoming a kind of independent domain, attached to the city proper at about this point but more and more a world apart. Few lived there and those who did not went there only when they couldn't help it, as when taking the North Wall emigrants' boat to England.

It is notable that Joyce, who set *Ulysses* all over central Dublin and some of its inner suburbs, sets none of its main action east of Butt Bridge. There are a few exceptions, such as the anecdote about Reuben J. Dodd, the hated moneylender to whom they were all in hock at one time or another, rewarding a boatman who fished his son out of the river, frustrating a despairing but failed suicide attempt after a failed love affair, with a nugatory, miserly sum. But that story is told in the mourning coach conveying Simon Dedalus and three others to Paddy Dignam's interment in Glasnevin Cemetery. At the moment Martin Cunningham tells the story, the coach is passing Nelson Pillar in the middle of Sackville Street. The North Wall locale of the anecdote is by the way.

By the end of the nineteenth century, Butt Bridge marked, more or less, the eastern limit of urban expansion – excluding the alien docklands. A process that we can trace from the building of Bloody/Watling Street/O'More Bridge in the 1670s judders to a halt at the end of the 1870s. The urban core had reached its natural limit for the moment. At that point, naturally, no one knew what was coming, but it came anyway: Joyce's centre of paralysis – a description I think fair enough but overstated; a political revolution that saw large parts of the city centre wrecked and two of its finest buildings torched; and forty years of economic sclerosis under a native government. It's hardly to be wondered as to why the energy gave out.

But give out it did. There was considerable expansion in the suburbs, as middle-class areas filled in and working-class housing was built with public funds, mainly in the outer western suburbs, to relieve the hideous and insanitary tenement overcrowding down town. But the centre remained largely untouched and bereft of economic energy or of the vital ingredient that sustains it: confidence in the future. In the first sixty years of the twentieth century, only one building of distinction – Busáras, the central bus station – was built, just behind the Custom House on Beresford Place. It was at least an example of architectural modernism, designed by Michael Scott, a man of genuine talent and ability.

In this, it contrasted rather embarrassingly with what followed from the 1960s. Admittedly, it was a pretty disastrous decade for architecture everywhere, with Stalinist Brutalism to the fore, complemented by office-block mediocrity put up at the direction of ignorant and opportunistic property developers. But neither excuse will serve to forgive Liberty Hall, the new headquarters of the Irish Transport and General Workers' Union, beside the northern abutment of Butt Bridge at the end of Eden Quay. This was sacred soil for the union, because it was from here that James Connolly – strange, quixotic man – marched his tiny force to the

Protest at Beresford Place following the arrest of Count Plunkett in 1917, with Loopline Bridge prominent in view

GPO in Sackville Street on Easter Monday and began the 1916 Rising, after which nothing was ever, or could be, the same again. The original Liberty Hall had stood on this site, a squat little building originally built as a hotel. The gunship *Helga*, deployed by the British on the river just below Butt Bridge on George's Quay, made short work of it on the Wednesday of the Rising.

So when the union came to build itself a spanking new headquarters in the 1960s, it naturally chose this site. It is a visually sensitive site, not because its neighbours along Eden Quay are buildings of any particular merit, but because of its visible proximity to O'Connell Bridge on one side and the Custom House adjacent on the other. What got built – courtesy of a civil engineer; the union decided that it could do without an architect – was and remains hideous. It is what they call in Kerry a big *fás thook* of a thing – as you would describe a gangling, overgrown, ungainly youth – and ugly as sin. It is a tall – tall being the whole point, so that the union could show who had the biggest dick in town –

vertical box with a silly little wave motif on the top, presumably a marine symbol of some sort. I don't know. It is utterly out of proportion to its surroundings, although interestingly it received gushing compliments from Irish contemporary architectural and building journals on completion.[6]

It still stands, although there are plans to replace it. And for sure it needs replacing, for in less than sixty years it has not weathered well. It has proved hard to maintain. It is either draughty or too hot; the windows rattle; and its only merit is that when you are there, it is the one place in central Dublin where you can't see Liberty Hall. Some people say that it is the ugliest building in the urban core, a competitive category. That's as may be, but it is hardly the ugliest structure. That glittering prize must be reserved for the Loopline Bridge adjacent, immediately downriver of Butt Bridge and right beside it. It is to this ibex that I turn next, my heart heavy.

– ✿ –

TWELVE

LOOPLINE BRIDGE

O K, WE CAN all agree that it is ugly and intrusive. Famously, it blocks the view of the Custom House, the finest classical building in Dublin, from the city centre. But still, it was an answer to a genuine problem. Dublin had no *hauptbahnhof* or *stazione centrale*, a central railway station where all lines met. The biggest of the early companies, the Great Southern & Western, had its terminus at Kingsbridge (Heuston), away upriver to the west. But with the construction of the Liffey Viaduct (chapter 10) it got connected, if a bit clumsily, with the western line operated by the Midland Great Western, whose terminus was at Broadstone in the north-west central quadrant, and the much more important Belfast line operated by the Great Northern Railway, with its central terminus in Amiens Street (Connolly). So one way and another, all the trunk systems were connected by 1880. Except one: the line south to Wicklow and Wexford operated by the Dublin and South Eastern Railway (DSER). It stopped at the DSER's terminus at Westland Row (Pearse).

So while Dublin was clearly the umbilicus of the system, one of its essential lines was disconnected from the rest. It is worth remembering, at this point, just where we are in time. In 1879, when Butt Bridge was built and the other railway lines had all been spatchcocked together, the railway was the wonder of the age. There was no alternative – at least for the moment. Dunlop had not even invented the pneumatic tyre, although Robert Thomson had already registered a patent for one as early as 1846 which, for reasons unknown, never gained any commercial traction. So the essential precondition for something as simple, if ingenious, was still a decade away.

The internal combustion engine was even farther in the future, with its inevitable teething problems delaying its full social impact until the early twentieth century. So, for the moment, the railway had mobility to itself. It requires a considerable act of the imagination to recover the effect that this invention had on every community that it touched. It was not just the manner in which it created a national wholesale and retail economy or opened up remote places, hitherto effectively inaccessible, or even the manner in which it created imagined communities, so that the Catholics of the Antrim Glens could feel an affinity with those of the Dingle Peninsula previously absent. (This imagined community was a potent consolidating feature of all nationalisms.) It was more than all this. It was the greatest advance in human mobility since the ancient invention of the chariot.

More than fifty generations had passed since the death of Christ, and the life of men and women was cribbed and cabined by whatever distance their feet could carry them or, if of the elite, their horse or a stagecoach. Most people, we know, never ventured more than about ten kilometres from where they were born. You walked if you wanted to get around. The early Romantics were fairly typical. De Quincey, visiting Coleridge in Somerset in 1807, walked forty miles back to Bristol, starting at 10 p.m. and thinking nothing of it. Coleridge himself and Southey did the same walk in the other direction, stopping for an overnight along the way. Wordsworth also walked prodigious distances, not least because he held a sinecure as 'receiver of stamps' which necessitated the superintendence of subordinates scattered across a wide area. Nor did Wordsworth and the others welcome the new. Like many literary intellectuals – in France, for example, the great poetic modernist Baudelaire was a cultural pessimist, anathematising the advance of the industrial revolution – Wordsworth was also a cultural pessimist; in his case, he poured much energy into preserving, as far as he could, his beloved Lake District from the vulgar intrusions of urbanity and the hoi polloi.

Then suddenly, from the 1830s on, there was this stunning thing: the iron horse that could get you around at speeds previously unimaginable. In Ireland, by 1880, there was already in place a dense and impressive railway network. It was destined to grow ever more dense until 1914. But then, war, financial overreach and, critically, the commercial development of the internal combustion engine relegated it to secondary status.

In the meantime, rail was king. And clearly, as the network was focused on Dublin, the disconnection between the Dublin and South Eastern system and the rest of the lines grated on people. As usual, the idea of completing the link had been around for decades, even before the consolidation effected by the Liffey Viaduct. As early as 1848, very early in the doings, a military engineer called Richard Hieram Sankey, later knighted for impressive imperial service in the subcontinent and Australia,[1] proposed as follows:

a bridge of one arch over the Liffey to cross opposite and pass through the Dock premises at an elevation of 50 feet above the level of high water and approached on either side by an inclined plane at an ascent of one in twenty. A communication to be established by this bridge between the Kingstown and Drogheda railways.[2]

It was an idea before its time but its time came in the 1880s. By now, the Dublin and South Eastern had extended far south beyond Kingstown (Dún Laoghaire) and finally reached Wexford in 1872, twenty years behind schedule.[3]

The communications revolution largely stimulated by the coming of the railway meant an increase in the volume of mail passing back and forth between Britain and Ireland. This was the proximate reason for the building of the Loopline Bridge. Of course, the proposal met with the customary opposition; in view of what was actually erected, for once we may sympathise with the protesters. Once the principle was admitted, however, an attempt was made to ensure that it ran east, that is downriver, of the Custom House. This was deemed to present 'insuperable difficulties', as had the original proposal to locate Butt Bridge where it was finally sited. Maybe this time the reasons were cogent, for it was not sited there but west of the Custom House, where it sits now in all its hideous garb.

This prompted another protest by the great and the good, professional, commercial interests and academics, who in 1884 petitioned the lord mayor in terms noted by de Courcy:

> we request the Right Hon. the Lord Mayor to convene a public meeting of the citizens of Dublin at the Mansion House at an early day to consider the Dublin Railway

Connecting Bill at present before parliament and to take steps to prevent the permanent disfigurement of the city by the railway bridge and viaduct proposed to be erected across the river west of the Custom House.

To no avail; the thing was built, with William Martin Murphy, of whom we shall hear more anon, being one of the financial backers, across this as he was to be across every mass transport initiative in Dublin for the next thirty years. It is 118 metres in length, comprising steel lattice girders riveted together to create its criss-cross pattern. It sits on huge girders set into the bed of the river, looking like vast elephants' feet. De Courcy, a temperate man not given to extravagant verbiage, simply notes that 'it is not generally regarded as an elegant structure', which is about the mildest thing anyone has ever said about the Loopline Bridge. Moreover, both Pearson and Gilligan note that the building of the railway viaduct – and specifically the elephants' feet on which it rested, made further upriver navigation impossible, thus frustrating the purpose of the new swivel bridge adjacent.

To compound its ugliness, the west side of the bridge was soon plastered with advertisements. Interestingly the east side, looking downriver, attracted no such commerce for, as we saw, the vibrant city effectively ended here with the lower river given over ever more to the alien docklands. Not much point in advertising if there was no one to look at the ads.

To access it from Westland Row station, otherwise the end of the line for the Dublin and South Eastern, it was necessary to punch a hole through the elevated front of the station, throw a railway bridge across Westland Row itself and wrap the extended

A view from Bachelors Walk along Eden Quay and down river to Dublin Bay, c. 1897

line around the eastern margin of Trinity College, then across another bridge on Great Brunswick (Pearse) Street to reach the river and the Loopline Bridge. At the river's edge, a new commuter station was opened at Tara Street, and once over the bridge the line curved around to Amiens Street Station, where its three new platforms on the loop were adjacent to but separate from the four platforms in the main station. All lines then merged on the northerly exit from the station. Thus was the Dublin railway system finally integrated, albeit in a kind of Heath Robinson arrangement.

So there the Loopline Bridge stands today, serving a severely practical purpose in all its ugliness, a visual blight upon what should be one of the city's finest vistas, downriver from O'Connell Bridge. The bridge peeps into *Ulysses* as the location for the cabman's shelter beneath where Bloom and Stephen repair after the surreal events in Bella Cohen's brothel in nearby Nighttown (the Eumaeus episode, chapter 16 of 18). On a less elevated note, it even made its way into a ballad, 'The Ragman's Ball', which describes the goings-on at the ragmen's annual knees-up:

> Come listen to me for a while
> Me good friends one and all
> And I'll sing to you a verse or two
> About a famous ball
> Now the ball was given by some friends
> Who lived down Ash Street
> In a certain house in the Liberties
> Where the ragmen used to meet ...
> Of eating, we had plenty now
> As much as we could hold
> We drank Brady's Loopline porter
> Until 'round the floor we rolled
> In the midst of all the confusion
> Someone shouted for a song
> When up jumps oul John Lavin and sings:
> 'Keep rollin' your barrel along'.

The Loopline reference is obscure. It may refer to a pub called Brady's, situated near the bridge, which corked its own bottled porter. Cork-bottled porter had a high reputation among the cognoscenti. Bottled porter (single X) and stout (double X) was, until the 1970s, sometimes fixed with corks rather than caps. Old-timers used to say that the corked version was far superior to the capped. I only had a corked bottle once in one of the last – perhaps the very last – pub in Dublin to cork their own, Kavanagh's of Prospect Square, now universally known as the Gravediggers because it abuts onto the boundary wall of Glasnevin Cemetery.

Whether it was auto-suggestion or a young man's imagination, I thought it the finest bottle of stout I ever had.

On which happy recollection, we leave the Loopline Bridge behind and take a break.

— ❦ —

WATER BREAK

O F ITS NATURE, this book cannot cover all of modern Dublin. It is focused on the river and its immediate environs. But the city has grown away from this riverine core, spreading north and south. The DART – its one electrified commuter line – runs from Malahide in the north to Greystones in County Wicklow in the south. Malahide is of the city but not in it; it is separated from the continuous built-up area, which stops at Clongriffin/Northern Cross, by a sort of green belt that lies under the principal flight approach path to Dublin airport at Collinstown. Greystones is mentally even more semi-detached. To the east, the city is restrained only by the Irish Sea; to the west, it spills out beyond the M50 orbital motorway, oozing towards Kildare.

Most of this large space is untouched – cannot be touched – in this book. The suburban and exurban development of Dublin would require another book and I am definitely not the person to write it. It would, no doubt, make a very fine academic study. As it is, I know of only one book tracing the historical and geographical growth of a single suburb. That is the Royal Irish Academy's publication on Clontarf, edited with admirable scruple by the historian Colm Lennon. It is number one in a projected publishing *grand projet* to trace the major suburbs of Dublin in book form; it is a subset of the RIA's Irish Historic Towns Atlas series. If future volumes do indeed appear – if I sound dubious, it is not out of cynicism, but based on many years' experience as a publisher, knowing full well the difficulties of bringing any such projected series to conclusion – they will and should be based on Lennon's exemplary, pioneering model.

That would be good work but alas it is not my work. Instead, I am obliged not to wander too far from the Liffey without the book collapsing into incoherence. Yet this in turn presents a difficulty. All of what we think of as historic Dublin – the medieval core and the Georgian city – is close to the river and influenced by it. That is what normally gets written about again and again; it is also what visitors and tourists come to see. It is what the city likes to show off.

But most of the footprint of modern Dublin, for better or worse, extends way beyond this relatively compact core. As late as the 1830s, that was pretty well all of Dublin, snug in the embracing armatures of the two canals, with the river running horizontally through the middle. But the dating is suggestive: the 1830s saw the arrival of the railway. It transformed everything and Dublin began its suburban sprawl. Much later came the car, embraced with almost manic enthusiasm as a mark of growing material prosperity. Much of the twentieth-century outer development has been predicated on the car as the principal means of personal mobility. If not the car, then the bus, but one way and another mobility by road and not rail.

But when it all started, rail was new and was king and road did not begin its ascent until after World War I, and then only modestly compared with what came after the 1960s. That early development, stimulated by the railway, pushed the city beyond the boundaries of the canals, especially on the south side. This was compounded by the creation of semi-independent townships in these areas, for local taxation purposes, to which the commercial bourgeoisie of the decaying city fled in large numbers. In time, the railways were augmented by an excellent tram network which had a similar effect. The story of Victorian Dublin is one largely of decay and decline, something to which I gave some space in my previous book, *The Irish Difference*.

But I was conscious, even as I was writing, that there was a danger of over-egging that particular pudding. It is, after all, the conventional wisdom, and that can be all too easy to latch onto. To the extent that that criticism is merited, it cannot be put right here for the reason already stated: that it would necessitate my wandering miles away from the river, which I cannot do. If someone else wants to have a go, let them.

In fact, at least one person has had a go, and a very good go it is. This is Michael Barry, whose *Victorian Dublin Revealed: The Remarkable Legacy of Nineteenth-Century Dublin* is indeed a revelation. It is a highly and lavishly illustrated volume on this crucial era; its illustrations alone convey the sheer extent of the Victorian achievement. Modern Dublin is unimaginable without its red-brick, post-Georgian wrapping. Indeed, you can see the transition from Georgian to Victorian at Upper Leeson Street, where the late-Georgian houses – Craig reckoned that the style, although much diminished physically, did not end until around 1860 – yield to the Victorian red-brick streets such as Elgin Road and so on to Ballsbridge a bit to the east. To the south – and after the last gasp of late Georgian on Morehampton Road – a similar process takes us to Donnybrook. Likewise the transition towards Ranelagh to the west.

Happily, there is one area not only not distant from the river but right on it where the weight of Victorian achievement is visible. It is time for us to take our water break from the bridges, past what at the start of the twentieth century was the last of them, and go down to the docks.

The huge extension of the Dublin docklands in this period is an unavoidable aspect of any account such as this focused on the Liffey. The city simply wouldn't exist without the river and its enormous nineteenth-century expansion of riverine commerce, not to mention the infrastructure required to enable it. This is absolutely germane to any understanding of how the modern city came to be what it is. There were indeed impressive engineering triumphs hereabouts in the eighteenth century: just think of the Great South Wall, snaking all the way out to the Poolbeg Lighthouse – as considerable an achievement as any Georgian square. There was the development of the inner docks around George's Dock, hard by the Custom House. This was the start of the entire nineteenth-century growth of the docks, a process begun well before Victoria came to the throne. But the term Victorian is loosely employed to cover the entire nineteenth century, and it is in that sense that I use it here.

———

There had been constant work over the centuries to tame and corral the unruly river. In particular, by building quay walls the channel was narrowed and deepened, at least at high water. But as anyone detraining today at Heuston Station when the tide is out can see for themselves, the upper reaches of the tidal Liffey can present a sorry sight at low water.

Downriver, however, things improve. The river – never much more than modest – broadens estuarially on its final passage to the sea. None the less, it had always presented navigational problems, even before consideration of winds and tides was taken into account. The North and South Bull sandbars just outside the mouth of the river and the constant silting of the navigation channel that they induced were a menace for centuries. The Great South Wall (finally completed in the 1790s), with its dog leg halfway down to the Poolbeg Lighthouse, was intended to ameliorate that problem, at least on the south side, but there were contrary views as to what to do on the north side.

Various solutions were proposed, most famously that of Captain William Bligh – he of *Mutiny on the Bounty* fame – who was commissioned by the Directors of Inland Navigation, a temporary body established by the Irish administration to address these problems among others. Bligh conducted a very thorough survey of the bay and the harbour, correcting errant calculations in earlier surveys. He proposed an extension of the North Wall, to run parallel to the South Wall. This proposal was rejected in favour of one offered by two members of the port board, George Maqay and Leland Crosthwaite, whose alternative was a pier to run from the seafront at Clontarf out to a point opposite the Poolbeg, in order to create a pinch point at the entrance to the harbour. Not only would it stop sand working its way in from the North Bull, it would also scour the river channel on the ebb tide, acting as a natural dredging mechanism.[1]

It was accepted: the wall was built and a new, smaller green lighthouse erected at the end to mark the northern boundary of the navigation channel. It was complete by 1824 and we know it today simply as the Bull Wall. Moreover, it worked as planned. It didn't solve every problem, nor did it obviate the need for mechanical dredging, but it opened the way to the further development of the port.

It also had an uncovenanted bonus: by arresting the natural movement of the North Bull sands washing into the harbour, it meant that they had to go somewhere else, because they weren't about to stop shifting just because some clever engineers had decreed it. So they went up instead of out, and in a short while what eventually became the North Bull Island began to form, dry land standing proud above high water. It is now about 5 kilometres in length, occupies an area of about 285 hectares/705 acres and is nearly a kilometre wide from the inner channel that separates it from the Clontarf shoreline and the open strand on the other side. It is a nature reserve, a special protection area for birds, a UNESCO biosphere reserve and, alas, home to two golf courses. It is also a hugely popular leisure facility for walking and bathing. All this within a few kilometres of the centre of a capital city.

———

It really is extraordinary the extent of new city infrastructure put in place in the last quarter of the seventeenth century; it left a permanent mark on the face of the city thereafter. One such remains with us today in a name that, although familiar, is largely forgotten. This is Sir John Rogerson, whose south-bank quay on the river is with us still. Presumably it is too far downstream and too obscure to have prompted a name change at independence, leaving us with the euphonious if somewhat anachronistic moniker of Sir John Rogerson's Quay, which runs from the end of City Quay at the junction with Creighton Street all the way down to the end of the south quays where they meet the mouth of the Dodder and the old docks at the end of the Grand Canal, finally come to town having completed its course from Shannon Harbour just north of Banagher, County Offaly – where, incidentally, Trollope, of all improbable people, had found employment as a postal surveyor's clerk in 1841, which job, according to himself, he made a go of and set him up for his return to England and fame as a novelist.

Rogerson was a contemporary of Sir Humphrey Jervis and not at all unlike him. He was, like Jervis, English by blood, but born in the Netherlands. However, he was reared in Dublin and made his whole career there, being educated at Trinity. It is remarkable the number of pushy and ambitious English merchants and traders who injected such energy into the growing town from the 1670s onwards: you can see why Craig used 1660 as his *point de départ* in his classic study, because things really did move with unprecedented speed from that date. It marked the restoration of Charles II and thus the return to legitimate normality after the hiatus of the Cromwellian commonwealth. This stabilised things on the basis of a new order in Ireland, with English adventurers given grants of land and, in the case of Dublin, enticed to drive new developments forward.

Rogerson, who followed the classic path of merchant, property developer, city alderman, MP and lord mayor (1693–4), as well as various other public offices of trust, experienced a nasty bump in the road at the time of the so-called Glorious Revolution of 1688, which was really a *coup d'état* against the legitimate

king, James II. But James was a Roman Catholic who had just
fathered a legitimate male heir – thus securing a Catholic royal
succession – which, among other things, panicked the merchants
and financiers of London into dethroning and replacing him with
the Dutchman William III, reliably Protestant. Sir John emerged
from this imbroglio, settled in Ireland at the battles of the Boyne
and Aughrim, as a staunch supporter of the new Protestant,
Williamite interest. He had backed the winning side. In addition
to his many other property holdings, he was granted 133 acres
on the south shore of the Liffey running back from Ringsend
to City Quay on condition that he should embank this stretch,
the better to deepen the navigation channel. This he did, and
despite later renewals of the entire south quays below Butt Bridge
between 1870 and 1913, the entire quay bears his name to this
day. (The very last stretch was called Great Britain Quay, but for
some mysterious reason this name never stuck.)[2]

Other things happened along the Liffey in the years that
followed Rogerson's death in 1724, most notable among them
the building of the Hibernian Marine School, a fine, imposing
building on Sir John Rogerson's Quay just to the west of where
the Sam Beckett Bridge now crosses the river. It was a charitable
school established in the 1770s by the Hibernian Marine Society
(although it appears to have started life in Ringsend in the previous
decade) in order to educate 'the children of decayed seamen' – that
is children of indigent or deceased members of the Royal Navy
and the merchant marine. It is recorded in a quite wonderful
vista by Malton, only one of the now two lost views from his
sanitised but seductive oeuvre. By the mid-nineteenth-century, it
was wanting for pupils, then, having been burned down in 1872,
was re-established in a number of locales, including Clontarf

The Hibernian Marine School, Sir John Rogerson's Quay, 1795

on the north side.[3] It finally amalgamated with two other small Anglican schools in 1972 and settled on the edge of Clontarf under the consolidated name of Mount Temple. This is where the U2 quartet were educated, although it's far from a decayed seaman's boy that Bono has become.

The completion of the Custom House in 1792 marked the beginning of the heroic age of docklands development. In the decades immediately following, the Custom House Docks and, on the south shore, the Grand Canal Docks were regarded by contemporaries with wonder. But neither lasted long, being superseded quickly by further developments downriver, so quickened was the pace of port expansion in the nineteenth century. The constantly increasing size of shipping, followed later by the transition from sail to steam, drove these accelerations. The Custom House Dock was built to the east of the Custom House and was finished in 1796. It occupied a space marked forty years earlier by Rocque as Amory's Ground, terra firma. The eponymous Amory was one Jonathan, who was granted this part of the foreshore back in 1675 to reclaim what were then sloblands subject to tidal inundation.[4] This he did.

But they were under water again once the Custom House Dock was constructed over a century later. It in its turn did not last long, as mentioned above. It fell into disuse after the construction of George's Dock adjacent in 1821, being known later in the century simply as the Old Dock. It was eventually filled in in 1927 to accommodate Memorial Road, an extension of Beresford Place that completed its semi-circular curve from the river wrapping round the Custom House from Butt Bridge to reach it again at what is now the Talbot Memorial Bridge.[5] As for the naming of Memorial Road, there is no agreement as to what it memorialises. De Courcy states that it is all sailors out of Dublin who perished at sea; Bennett that it recalls the Dublin Brigade of the IRA who, with revolutionary zeal, burned the Custom House, the finest classical building in the city. Take your pick.

So by the time the Bull Wall was completed in 1824, the first generation of deep-water docks was likewise finished. That first generation didn't last long, as the expansion of the port gathered speed.

———

The North Wall from the Custom House down to where it turns north at East Wall was completed by the 1720s. It is shown on Brooking's map (1728) but more clearly on Rocque's (1756). It stood in constant need of repair until finally it was rebuilt in 1869.

During that time, the key positions in the port were held

successively by two men: George Halpin, who had no professional qualifications but was a supremely practical man, a builder by trade, and his son George Halpin Jnr, who was a qualified engineer. The job of port engineer doubled up with that of inspector of lighthouses, and it was while on duty in this latter connection that the elder Halpin died, both jobs passing to the son. Between them, they had made many improvements along the North Wall, providing deeper berthages for ever-larger shipping, warehouses for goods – all the more important now that the railways were arriving and creating a national retail economy, thus necessitating central distribution depots – and graving (or dry) docks for ship repairs. The younger Halpin's assistant left in 1856 and was replaced by a young engineer with the unusual name of Bindon Blood Stoney. As Halpin Jnr was engrossed in his lighthouse works, Stoney became de facto the port engineer, succeeding formally to the title in 1868 and holding the position with the greatest possible distinction for thirty years.

Stoney had been born in Queen's County (Offaly) in 1828, a younger son. His unusual name referred to his maternal grandfather, Bindon Blood. There is, alas, no firm evidence to link him to the famous Captain Thomas Blood (1618–80), the scapegrace and adventurer best remembered for his attempt at stealing the Irish crown jewels from the Tower of London, other than that both men were apparently born in County Clare, although obviously generations apart. That is hardly enough, which is a pity.

At any rate, his grandson took his name along with his father's, thus Bindon Blood Stoney. He qualified as a civil engineer at Trinity and worked first for Lord Rosse at Parsonstown (Birr), then in Spain and then back in Ireland as the resident engineer – but not the designer – on the huge railway viaduct over the

Boyne at Drogheda. This was quite rightly considered a wonder of the age. His work here made him a pre-eminent international authority on load- and weight-bearing structures, which eventually led to the publication in 1866 of his standard textbook on the subject, bearing one of those verbose Victorian titles that make us smile today: *The THEORY OF STRESSES in Girders and Similar Structures with Practical Observations of the Strength and Other Properties of Materials*, which simply became known to civil engineering students everywhere as Stoney on Stresses. In the course of a long career in Dublin Port, he was involved in such works as the strengthening of the Poolbeg Lighthouse and of many of the Liffey bridges, not least O'Connell Bridge, as we saw in chapter 7, and the deepening of berthages along the North Wall. New buildings along the North Wall testify to the developments he superintended: the Railway Hotel, a red-brick structure that served as the terminus hotel for passengers arriving from Holyhead on the service run by the London and North Western Railway Company, which had the franchise to run the Holyhead packet service from Britain, still stands there, rather forlorn and orphaned now. But it was Stoney's pioneering work in the use of pre-cast concrete blocks, weighing up to 350 tons, employing a floating crane and a diving bell to install these monsters in the riverbed at low water (he became known as 'the father of Irish concrete', surely one of the least enviable – if well deserved – epithets in history), that secured his celebrity.

People in the know did not smirk. Stoney was awarded the Telford Medal in 1874, was elected a Fellow of the Royal Society and was confidently predicted to be knighted, although that bauble never came. It might have done, because it was his genius that saw the North Wall extension – everything in the modern port

east of East Wall Road down to the open sea, Alexandra Basin
and all, and bounded to the north by Promenade Road looking
across the inner channel to Clontarf – completed. Given that the
Prince of Wales and his missus, after whom the basin was named,
performed the official opening, you'd think that the least they
could have done was to make a knight of this distinguished man.[6]

Bindon Blood Stoney is hardly remembered today in Dublin.
Stoney Road in East Wall commemorates him, and a short and
rather undistinguished street near Hanover Quay bears his full
name. His memory surely deserves better from the city than that.
He was one of Dublin's eminent Victorians – I use the term
soberly and not at all in the sneering manner of Lytton Strachey's
original – for there were a number of them. In a previous book, I
was rather harsh on the smallness of the overall achievement in
the city in that era. Perhaps that's why the achievements of people
like Stoney stand in such clear historical relief.

I am also thinking of heroic figures such as Sir Charles
Cameron (1831–1921) who was chief medical officer of Dublin
Corporation for more than fifty years, waging a constant war
against slum landlords, adulterers of food and beer, and an
officialdom indifferent to the exploitation of the poor. Likewise,
Sir John Gray (1816–75), proprietor and editor of the influential
Freeman's Journal, the principal nationalist newspaper of the time.
After an early career in medicine, which he abandoned for public
life, his position as an influential editor gave him the leverage to
help institute the Dublin fire brigade and the cattle market on the
North Circular Road. But his greatest achievement was the Vartry
Water Scheme in the second half of the 1860s. This brought a
supply of clean drinking water at high pressure from the River
Vartry in County Wicklow via a reservoir at Stillorgan, outside the

south city suburbs at the time. Of all the schemes proposed for the city, the Vartry option was the most expensive. But it was the one that went ahead, thanks in large part to Gray's political nous and clout. It placed laggardly old Dublin well ahead of most British cities of the time in this if in nothing else and was probably the greatest single achievement of the nineteenth-century corporation. And at least Gray was remembered, unlike poor Cameron, with a statue that stands in the middle of O'Connell Street to this day.[7]

Stoney was of that ilk: a difficult man, if records are to be believed, but in the bull-headed, self-assured way of the Victorian improving expert. Nineteenth-century Dublin could have done with a few more like him and Cameron and Gray.

THIRTEEN

TALBOT MEMORIAL BRIDGE

W ELCOME TO THE age of the car. Of the eight bridges built since the late 1970s, five have been for traffic relief (which, in the modern world, means cars in ever-growing numbers), two for pedestrian use only and one principally for public transport.

Growth in car ownership, especially private car ownership – not counting trucks, lorries and other commercial vehicles depending on the internal combustion engine – is a sure sign of growing prosperity. This is simply a sociological fact. Whether it is desirable or not, which in some respects it is not, it is undeniably the wish of a population experiencing material advance and expanding personal disposable income. In this, it is similar to developments in other countries. It is also similar to the growth of domestic consumer goods: washing machines, televisions, central heating systems and so forth. In 1952, when the late Queen Elizabeth ascended the throne of the United Kingdom, there were hardly any houses that had telephones, while outside toilets were still common. And that was in rich Britain, or at least rich compared to Ireland.

In Greater Dublin, just to focus on car ownership, since that is most material to what follows, the great increase in private car registrations from 1961 – roughly the beginning of the end of the post-war economic sclerosis – drove public policy, partly because transport policy followed consumer demand but also because there was little cultural and political commitment to the development of a European-style public transport system. We have already seen how the urban railway system is really a kind of arse-patching, bolting together the residual bits of the infrastructure put in place by the Victorians. Consumer demand was for the car, and politicians and planners followed that demand by providing principally for the car.

Advocates for public transport have been on the back foot for the best part of the past fifty years, although they have recovered their position somewhat in more recent times. Overall, however, this has been an age of new money, consumerism and individualism. In transport terms, that means the autonomy and comfort afforded by owning one's own car and relying on it disproportionately for personal mobility.

As if this trend required any further stimulus, the demand for low-density private housing, three-bedroom semi-detached houses with gardens fore and aft in ever-spreading suburbs, reinforced it. It was all very well to complain about little boxes and the unsustainability of private transport. The property developers, themselves men (nearly always men) of rough provincial origin who, for the greater part, had little 'feel' for urbanity and absolutely no cultural commitment to such sentimental nonsense, argued, and they were not wrong, that their sprawling little boxes colonising the growing suburbs were merely answering consumer demand. They were giving their customers what those customers most desired.

King George IV entering Dublin in 1821. Heuston (King's) Bridge was constructed to commemorate the first peaceful visit to Ireland by a British Monarch in 650 years.

Rather than welcoming royalty, nowadays Heuston Bridge carries the LUAS Red Line.

A view of the Dublin and Kingstown Railway, looking across Dublin Bay towards Williamstown and Merrion, with Dublin in the distance, 1834.

The Ha'penny Bridge was the first purpose-built pedestrian bridge in Dublin.

Considerably below street level, the Liffey Viaduct is the bridge that nobody sees.

The Loopline (as per usual) blocking the view of the Custom House from the city centre, with Butt Bridge in the foreground.

Matt Talbot Memorial Statue with bridge and the Custom House in the background.

Dublin Port at night as seen from the East Link Bridge.

Opened in 1999 to mark the close of the twentieth century, the Millennium Bridge was only the second pedestrian crossing over the Liffey.

James Joyce's most famous short story 'The Dead' takes place in 15 Usher's Island (*left of centre*), directly opposite the south side of James Joyce Bridge.

The Seán O'Casey Bridge links the International Financial Services Centre on the north bank to City Quay on the south.

An old Dublin tram from Howth Transport Museum placed on Rosie Hackett Bridge for the official opening, 20 May 2014.

The Samuel Beckett Bridge makes its way from Rotterdam to Dublin,
March 2009.

Samuel Beckett Bridge is the most aesthetically stunning of the Liffey's twenty river bridges,
and the Dublin Convention Centre (*right*) isn't too shabby either.

Aerial view of the River Liffey from Rosie Hackett Bridge eastwards.

Thus the huge sprawl of west Dublin at that time. And if you lived out in your bijou box on the new edge of the city, you needed to get back in to get to work. And the easiest way to do that – and the one most desired – was to have one's own car. It reached a point where public transport, most obviously the bus service, was regarded as a poor person's option and private commuting a sign of independence and social advance. That has changed a bit in recent times with the growth of green consciousness, the huge improvements in the bus system, the construction of the successful Luas on-street tram system and a renewed interest in and commitment to the humble bicycle.

But still, the dominance of the car has remained the principal leitmotif of urban transport policy, which brings us to a classic example of the tragedy of the commons. What is good for the individual is bad for the communality. Roads simply couldn't be built fast enough to accommodate the huge growth in car ownership and the twice-daily dependence on motorised commuting to get around the place. No matter how many roads were built, including the orbital M50, the available space simply could not cope with the ever-expanding demand. Thus the horrors of crawling through suburban traffic, as thick and slow as treacle, while watching with something not far short of anger cyclists whizzing through at faster speeds – maddeningly ignoring things like red traffic lights while projecting, wittingly or otherwise, an air of smug superiority – caused frustration and road rage. Anyone who has had this experience will recognise this summary.

In addition, this emphasis on roads and private transport – and remember, this was a cultural choice, based on expressed consumer preference to which politicians of all kinds were ultra-sensitive in a populist democracy – was not just some sort of malign conspiracy.

There was never much of a market anywhere in Ireland, and certainly not in Dublin, for social democratic planning. The calibre of political candidates returned at local and national elections is plain testament to that. Like the builders, the politicians, with the planners in tow, were simply giving the public what it wanted. Populist, localist, glib short-term 'solutions' to complex long-term problems were the order of the day, all day every day. They got you elected, ya daarlin' man.

Sadly, it also entailed some ugly urban road building and widening, sometimes in spaces that were ill-deserving of such vandalism. It aggregated to a series of ad hoc expedients, often greased by corruption in the planning process, and all ultimately dependent on private transport.

And so it went on. The only conspicuous exception to the general trend was the electrification of Dublin's one coastal railway – part of the Belfast main line to Malahide on the north side, with an existing branch to Howth, and of the Wexford main line to Greystones in the south. This was the DART (from 1984), for the most part a middle-class luxury, although, to the extent that it was, it at least provided a genuine public transport alternative in areas of densest car ownership. But overall the direction of travel, so to speak, was clear.

From 1879 to 1978, Butt Bridge was the last bridge on the lower Liffey. As mentioned in chapter 11, when the bridge was finally approved it was intended to build another one just downstream, on the east side of the Custom House. This never got built, and that remained the case until the Matt Talbot Memorial Bridge was erected in the latter year. The reason, once again, was traffic. The sheer weight of urban traffic necessitated turning Butt Bridge into a one-way carriageway, south to north, which required the

Talbot Memorial Bridge with the Custom House behind

construction of a new bridge to accommodate cross-river traffic going north to south.

The Talbot Bridge has no particular architectural merit. It was not architect designed, although architects were consulted on specific aspects of the work. It was the first Liffey bridge to be constructed mainly of pre-stressed concrete, thus nodding to the memory of Bindon Blood Stoney, and it may be said of it that it is inoffensive, discreetly pleasing to the eye, and that by maintaining its modest appearance and low-slung triple span it does not interfere with views of the Custom House from downriver. From north to south, it leads straight on to Moss Street, but this is a nondescript street which attracts little traffic. Instead, vehicles divide left and right on the south side, left for the lower quays, Westland Row and Merrion Square – thus bypassing the central clutter – and right for the southern quays going west and for the city centre.

In a city whose whole transport policy was centred on the private car, the Talbot Bridge made every sense at the time of its construction. But that car-orientated policy was itself flawed. Even so, it has established itself as a vital part of the centre-city infrastructure. How it might be adapted for future plans remains to be seen.

It is named for Matt Talbot (1856–1925), a recovered alcoholic who was for years a casual labourer for the port board and later worked in the private sector. From a young age, he had been a very heavy drinker. But at the age of twenty-eight, he took a pledge of total abstinence and returned to his religious duties, which he had neglected in his drunken years. He practised severe personal mortification, including body chains, which were only discovered after his death. He was emaciated; he collapsed and died in Granby Lane, off Parnell Square. In an age of piety, his example of personal redemption was regarded as heroic, and he was awarded the title of 'servant of God' by the Catholic Church, a potential first step towards canonisation.

Later generations have been less kind, as Ireland progressively secularised. In the 1980s, he was remembered by the impious as Boney M, a play on the name of a contemporary pop group which specialised in funky vocals. It is doubtful if, in the current post-religious climate, anything – let alone anything as prominent and permanent as a bridge – would be named for him. But the bridge's naming is none the less a reminder that a very different Ireland, with a sensibility ever more remote from our own, is not long in the past.

– ✿ –

FOURTEEN

FRANK SHERWIN BRIDGE

ANOTHER ROAD BRIDGE, built for cars, named for one just as obscure today as Matt Talbot – indeed, even more so. Without conducting a vox pop, I'd guess that some people under forty might make a stab at the identity of Talbot but I doubt that many, if any, of them could say a single thing about Frank Sherwin. A footballer, maybe, or an old music-hall turn from long ago at the Theatre Royal?

None of the above.

Frank Sherwin (1905–81) was a local politician, regarded at the time – when standards in this department were not too challenging – as a colourful character. This derived from his natty suits and his fondness for bow-ties and trilby hats. Sherwin was born poor, one of eleven, in Dorset Street. Along with Frank, only one other sibling made old bones, with six of the other nine dying in childhood. He left school at thirteen and assumed republican views which he never abandoned, fighting for the Irregulars in the Civil War. He spent some time in a number of detention centres and was finally released in 1924.

Sherwin may have come from an impoverished background but he quickly discovered a flair for business. He established himself in the dance-hall business, a good choice at the time when Ireland, newly independent but puritanical in its mores, was rife with stringent literary censorship and growing episcopal hysteria about sex and communism, neither of which were conspicuous by their presence in the holy island. People needed some sort of relief from this suffocating Puritanism and found it in dancing and the cinema, each of which attracted the Irish public in astonishing numbers.

Sherwin surfed this wave and at the height of his business success was the proprietor of no fewer than twenty-seven dance halls in the Greater Dublin Area.[1] By the mid 1950s, he was ready to enter public life. He stood as an independent candidate for the Dublin Corporation, serving from 1955 to '67 and again from 1974 until his death. He was a populist in the finest Irish tradition, a glad-hander, a crowd-pleaser and a localist who took short views. His principal interests were urban housing for the poor, social welfare payments and partition.

He might have remained a minor local character were it not for his election to the Dáil in a by-election in 1957, retaining his inner-city north-side seat in the general election of 1961. It was this that propelled him into brief national fame. After that election, Fianna Fáil under Seán Lemass formed a minority government, dependent on the votes of friendly independents for its parliamentary majority. Sherwin, with his republican background, was more sympathetic to Fianna Fáil than any other major party (he had been a founder member in 1926 but later fell out with the party), and it was this inclination that brought him to wider public notice.

The government proposed a novel 2.5 per cent turnover tax – a form of Value Added Tax – on certain goods and services. This caused tremendous controversy and Lemass's government would fall if the well-disposed independents did not support it. They came under severe public and parliamentary pressure not to do so, but they did in numbers sufficient to deliver a comfortable majority for the proposal in the end. Sherwin was one of these, arguing that the revenue thus raised could fund higher welfare payments for the poor. This cost him his Dáil seat in 1965; he never regained it. It also cost him his corporation seat, accounting for his absence from that body from 1967 to 1974, when he only scraped back in by the skin of his teeth.

Sherwin was no liberal. He had – let us be charitable here – antique views on women in general and specifically in public life. He was sympathetic to the Provisional IRA on its formation in 1970, offering this 'solution' to the fast-deteriorating Northern Ireland problem: 'the solution to the northern problem is for the British Army to get out ... The Orangemen would not last a week against the northern nationalists supported by southern government. If the Orangemen did fight it would be a good thing in the long run as it would clear the northern area of foreign bigots.' Nor did he have any time for the local Travelling community, describing them as professional beggars and burglars.

But he claimed, none the less, to be a moderniser. He deplored the network of narrow streets in central Dublin and, despite his frequently expressed concern for the interests of local residents, did not scruple to support the solutions proposed by the city transport engineers, which resulted in road-widening schemes that gashed through North King Street, Summerhill and the Patrick Street/Nicholas Street areas. These schemes primarily served the interests

The official opening of Frank Sherwin Bridge, 1982

of car users rather than the local population, although Sherwin did support the replacement accommodation built for them – low-rise suburban-style terraced and semi-detached houses that looked out of place in the central urban milieu. As with all populists, Frank knew what the people wanted and helped to give it to them.

All of which explains why the new bridge thrown across the river near Heuston Station was named for him in the year after his death, a sentimental nod to the memory of a colourful if not always well-beloved local character.

The bridge was necessitated, as always in this period, by increasing traffic. The original King's Bridge (Heuston Bridge after the renaming of 1966) was no longer able to bear the weight of traffic using it. So the new bridge, taking traffic from the south to the north quays, was built right beside it. Yet another low-slung, three-span reinforced concrete structure, it is inoffensive to the eye. It is also almost unique among all the Liffey bridges in that it has had no impact, good or bad, on urban development either side of it. It is simply there to accommodate traffic movement, all very well in its way given the realities of the time and the absence of any serious commitment to public transport provision, but really that's as much as can be said about it.

Ironically, when public transport eventually came higher on the agenda of the city authorities, it brought the old, abandoned Heuston Bridge back into play. It now accommodates one of the two Luas tram lines, opened in 2004. Here the line crosses the river, thus connecting Heuston and Connolly Stations.

– ❀ –

FIFTEEN

EAST LINK

THIS IS THE last bridge on the river before the open sea. It dates from 1984 and, once again, it has to do with traffic flow. It is, in effect, an eastern relief route. In that sense, it follows the same logic as Butt Bridge and the Talbot Memorial Bridge upriver, taking vehicular traffic away from the centre to relieve pressure on the urban core. A similar logic lay behind the building of the M50 orbital motorway to the west of the city (1983–2010). It girdles three sides of the city, from the port right around to north County Wicklow. But it has never completed a circular embrace of Dublin on the eastern or seaward side, principally because there are too many established built-up suburbs in the proposed way of it, especially on the south side. It would have entailed the destruction of about 100,000 houses and the obliteration of Sandymount Strand. Various routes were proposed over many years, but all came up against the same objection. It was not abandoned until as late as 2021, when the planning emphasis was on more public transport provision, a greater awareness of sustainability and green issues generally, and a recognition that new roads provided no more than a temporary patch-up, because the experience of other excessively car-dependent cities was that added road capacity soon filled up, landing the city more or less back where it started in the first place – and all at an eye-watering cost to the public purse.

The planning attitude at the time was summed up by George Redmond, who ended up as assistant city manager before being convicted of accepting bribes from developers. This, from 1979:

> You can't put restraints on car ownership – politically, it's just not on. Motorists feel that they have a God-given right to drive where they please and there is no political will to stop them. It is a question of individual freedom and they won't have it taken away. Ever since Adam and Eve, it's been the same story.[1]

It took decades to demonstrate the futility of this thinking, and although the alternative – improved public transport provision – has happened, the underlying problem still remains: Dublin is too car dependent and the full cost of bringing the public transport system up to something like standards prevailing in France, Belgium and Germany, whether by fixed rail, trams or buses or some mixture of the three, is still formidable. At any given moment, the city can't afford it.

So by the mid 1980s, the emphasis was still on providing for the private car. (The one benign exception was the electrification rail project that created the DART, as mentioned in chapter 13.) Thus the requirement for an eastern relief crossing of the lower Liffey. The initiative came from Tom Roche, an industrialist, who proposed a toll bridge, a relatively novel idea in Dublin (and in Ireland) at the time, although a commonplace now on major routes. The government gave Roche the go-ahead to construct a bridge from Thorncastle Street in Ringsend to the junction of the North Wall and East Wall Road. This he did. Within a year, over a million vehicles had used the new bridge. So the planners' analysis was not all wrong: clearly, the demand was there, if only for want of an alternative.

However, it had to be an opening bridge, as the original Butt Bridge had been and for the same reason. Port shipping still required access to the parts of the river west of the bridge, up towards the city. So the central section of this four-span structure, which is over 200 metres in all from one wall of the river to the other, is a 33-metre opening span. The effect, when opened, is dramatic: the section rises like a huge stiff-arm salute at an angle of about 40 degrees to the horizontal. It can be raised in about one minute, and the estimated time required for one ship to pass through the opening is about three and a half minutes.[2]

It is officially called the Tom Clarke Bridge, in memory of one of the leaders of the 1916 Rising, but no one calls it that. It replaced a number of ferries that plied the lower river.

It is not without its problems. Not the least of them is the journey from south to north at times of maximum traffic pressure, especially during rush hours. The single-carriageway approach road billows out into three lanes, each of which has a toll booth, before contracting again to a single lane on the approach to the bridge. This is a certain recipe for traffic jams, and sure enough they happen. A great deal of jostling and lane infiltration is required, inevitably done at a snail's pace, to get everyone in turn into the single lane to carry them north across the bridge. The odd bridge opening, by contrast, seldom produces a long delay, but the three-into-one squeeze invariably does.

The British tall ship *Pelican of London* sailing through the raised East Link Bridge

The bridge led to an upgrade of the East Wall Road to accommodate northbound traffic, in particular traffic headed for the nearby Port Tunnel and the airport. This means that south siders can get to the airport without having to look at too much of the north side, a benison for the poor lambs. It also throws an extra weight of traffic headed for the northern suburbs – Clontarf and adjoining areas – once the road makes a 90-degree turn to wrap around the eastern edge of East Wall itself.

As to the Port Tunnel, it opened in 2006 to run from just north of that turn on the East Wall Road to join with the eastern end of the M50, the nearby airport and the M1 motorway to Northern Ireland. It was originally intended as a relief road for commercial traffic coming in and out of the port via the M50, thus taking the vast majority of heavy goods vehicles and huge articulated trucks out of the inner suburbs and the city centre. In this, it has been a considerable success. It subsequently opened to all vehicles. It runs under some north-side suburbs, prompting alarm about possible damage to houses and subsidence. This threat proved exaggerated, if not non-existent. After all, Paddy had been digging ditches and tunnels for half the world for ages. Why not build one for himself?

———

The East Link has made its own contribution to the development of the lower Liffey, on both banks. While the earliest modern development was the International Financial Services Centre (IFSC), running from Memorial Road down as far as Commons Street, a compact enough area, it spread out from there. The IFSC set new standards for integrated architectural design in the city, and some of the buildings here, roughly on the site of the old Spencer Dock, are genuinely impressive and visually pleasing.

The IFSC got itself a bad name during the days of the roaring Celtic Tiger as a kind of Wild East of finance capitalism. There is an irony here, because while many of the charges laid against the centre were well founded – many brass-plate operations and other shadowy and dubious accommodations – the whole thing was a prompt for the more structured development of the lower quays in general. Thus an exercise in let-it-rip capitalism helped to anchor subsequent developments that were much more social democratic in character.

For this, we can thank government. Ruairí Quinn of the Labour Party was minister for finance in a coalition government from 1994 to 1997. It was he whose initiative led to the upgrading of the Custom House Docks Development Authority, originally established in 1986 and under whose aegis the IFSC was developed. Its initial remit had been confined to the site of the original IFSC.

However, under legislation piloted through by Quinn, the Dublin Docklands Development Authority Act 1997, its practical scope was greatly extended and now covered both sides of the river.[3]

What followed was a series of developments, mixing private and public sectors and largely driven by the authority. The riverside has been transformed on both banks, although there is still a stark contrast between this riverine membrane and the long-established working-class areas just behind. That said, the authority made it its business from the beginning to consult and involve the established local community. This was, understandably, met with some considerable initial suspicion. The contrast between well-tailored planners and architects, all invincibly suburban and middle class, and the existing inner-city lower working-class community was stark. Sheriff Street, just behind the glittering north bank membrane, remains one of the poorest communities in Ireland. That said, it has seen a degree of public investment in this area – and in similar south-side areas near the dockside developments – that has delivered huge improvements in social cohesion, educational opportunities, a frank addressing of problems generated by illegal drugs and so on.

That is why I refer to what has happened along the quays as an exercise in social democracy. It is not hostile to free-market capitalism, but the authority has taken seriously its obligations under statute to bring existing local communities along with it. It took time to engender trust, understandably. But the results have been genuinely impressive and might very well set an example for the intelligent renewal of other neglected areas. Perhaps, after all, there is more to this kind of thing than the pitiless bullying of a Baron Haussmann, who would simply have turfed everyone in Sheriff Street out on their ears, invited them to make their own arrangements and built a boulevard. In short, the whole thing is an exercise in temperate planning.

It even extends as far downriver as the East Link. The bridge opened up possibilities on both banks simply by providing the crossing: the link. Immediately on the north bank lay the site of the old Point Depot, which we met in chapter 10. It had lain disused for years once abandoned as a railway storage depot. This was converted into a concert venue, the Point Theatre, in 1988, with a capacity of over five thousand, and during the nineties and noughties it became a major venue on the international circuit. It has since gone through a couple of mutations and operates at present as the 3Arena.

The area immediately behind it, at the eastern end of Upper Sheriff Street, has had mixed fortunes. It was developed, principally by the enterprising Harry Crosbie, as the Point Village, but it ran into the headwinds of the financial crash of 2008 and subsequent years, which silenced the roar of the Celtic Tiger. None the less, the progress that has been made is palpable – and accessible, especially since the red line of the Luas tramway was extended there in 2009.

Apart from bad luck with the financial crash, the Point Village development has suffered from something similar to Smithfield upriver: a reluctance to move too much of urban activity from the old central core. Like Smithfield, it has a half-finished feel, not possessed of the constant throb and press of people that characterises the city centre. Fans coming to performances in the 3Arena go home afterwards. The area has been hugely improved, with much potential for further initiatives, but the sense of 'provide it and they will come' is absent.

None the less, for anyone who can, as I can, remember the

area before all these things happened, what has eventuated – all the way down from Memorial Road to the East Link – is a near-miraculous transformation. The balance sheet is hugely positive, and there is much for future generations to build on further. We'll see more on these benign developments in chapters 18 and 19.

————

On the south side, there has been one surprising and almost certainly unintended consequence of the building of the East Link Bridge. The access road to reach it was created anew with an approach road named for Seán Moore, as was a public park adjacent at the Sandymount end of the approach road. Moore was a local politician, a former lord mayor of the city and briefly government chief whip under Charles Haughey's first administration from 1979. He was a nice man, a harmless localist glad-hander in the classic tradition of Irish local government. What all these roads did was to improve, if only slightly, access from this point to the Great South Wall. It certainly brought this astonishing structure into greater public focus. Access to it is still by small roads – so cars and bicycles only – through container-laden dockland marshalling yards, a sewage works, past the old Pigeon House and beneath the shadow of the twin chimneys built for the Poolbeg electricity-generating station. They have become part of the city's iconic urban furniture.

In fact, your journey to the city end of the Great South Wall entails a traverse of all the reclaimed land to the east of Ringsend, covering part of the old South Bull sandbank. At the end is the wall, jutting out into the harbour down to the distant red landmark of the Poolbeg Lighthouse, over three kilometres away.

The story of the South Wall began in 1707 and the whole structure was not complete until the 1790s. This means that not one of the people who put the entire thing in motion lived to see it complete. Yet the work continued through the eighteenth century, with mistakes, wrong turns and all the customary muddle, yet it was persisted with to create one of the most effective breakwaters – and certainly one of the most visually arresting – anywhere.

In 1707 there was passed 'An Act for Cleansing the Port, Harbour and River of Dublin and for erecting a Ballast Office in the said city'. This was the legislation enabling the establishment of the city's first port authority under municipal control. (Previously, such functions had been the direct responsibility of the crown.) Ballast is any substance – gravel or similar – placed in the keel of an otherwise unladen merchant ship to ensure its stability. By extension, a Ballast Office superintends the contents of ships entering and departing a port. The key functions of this first one were the imposition of port charges and the maintenance of the navigation channel. Therein lay an ancient problem: the vulnerability of the harbour to silting, given the vigour and distance covered by the six-hourly tides and the abundance of sand on the North and South Bull sandbanks ready to be washed into the central channel.

By the 1720s, the embanking of the north side of the Liffey down to the end of the North Wall – where the northern abutment for the East Link Bridge now stands – was complete. But already the port authority had turned its attention to the south shore. It began the building of what eventually became the Great South Wall as early as 1716. First it tried timber piles pushing out towards the Poolbeg lightship, as it was at the time, but the structure was too rickety to survive the tides. The constant

Poolbeg Lighthouse with Howth Head in the distance, 1842

repairing and maintenance of the breakwater was a self-defeating labour of Sisyphus. Moreover, the lightship itself, away in the distance, was insecure. It was proposed to replace it with a fixed lighthouse as early as 1736 and again in 1744. But in the classic way of many public projects in the history of the city, as we have repeatedly seen in this book, every excuse was found for not doing the obvious.

Finally, in 1759 it was settled. The lightship became the Poolbeg Lighthouse that we know today; it was completed in 1767. In the meantime, a solid wall known as the Ballast Office Wall had been built east from Ringsend, and in 1761 there began the work of extending this wall further east along the line of the unsatisfactory timber piles – in effect replacing them – to the lighthouse. They worked from the lighthouse back towards the city, so that the western end of the wall – where the car- or bicycle-borne visitor meets it today – was the last bit completed. But by the 1790s it was all in place. The timber piles had been replaced by great granite blocks, 9.5 metres wide at the bottom and 8.3 metres at the top. The whole thing stands 1.6 metres above high water.[4]

To walk the Great South Wall today is rather like walking on water, figuratively. This long snaking breakwater extending deep into the harbour below the mouth of the river is one of the delights of the city, but unknown to many. At that, the building of the East Link – or at least of the road infrastructure connecting to it – did bring this fabulous amenity into greater public consciousness. On the south side, you can see the sweep of the shore from the mountains back into Sandymount; on the northern side, from the hill of Howth back into Clontarf and Fairview. Also, shipping in and out of the port comes very near. At the end, standing beneath the lighthouse, look east: there is nothing but salt water between you and Anglesey.

One other thing that the bridge did was to leave Ringsend alone. There is no direct road access from the south side of the bridge to this ancient and very distinct urban village, even though it is right nearby. If you want to get there, you have to go the long way round, unless of course you are on foot, in which case a narrow walkway carries you into York Road and Thorncastle Street. You will be following in the footsteps of many, including Oliver Cromwell, who came ashore here in 1649 sick as a dog after his first-ever sea voyage.

— ❦ —

SIXTEEN

MILLENNIUM BRIDGE

T LAST, A pedestrian bridge. Until this bridge was put in place in 1999, there was only one pedestrian crossing over the Liffey, the Ha'penny Bridge just upstream (chapter 8). That dated from 1816. On the lower river, there were ferries across the wider waterway until the East Link and other new bridges below the Custom House were built either side of the millennium. Ferries had operated on the Liffey from the time that the old Church Street Bridge had collapsed in 1385 and was not replaced for more than forty years (chapter 1, p. 18). The last of the ferries downriver lasted until the completion of the East Link, finally ending a tradition of centuries.

The Millennium Bridge, as its name suggests, was planned as part of the city's farewell to the twentieth century and its welcome to the twenty-first. An earlier proposal for a bridge on this site had not met with approval, so when it was resolved to build something here, it was thrown open to Irish and international competition. The successful entry, out of 153 submitted, came from Howley Harrington, an Irish architectural practice, with Price & Myers as consultant engineers. I mention the engineers because their contribution to the finished product was essential.

The bridge has a span of 41 metres. That's all: the Liffey is a modest river, at least until below Butt Bridge when it does begin to billow, as the open sea beckons. This is no Thames or Seine and it invites no grandiloquent pontine extravagance. The Millennium Bridge is perfect, in my eyes the most successful and discreet of all the Liffey crossings. It does not *announce* itself: there are no trumpet blasts here, but something instead more like the hardly noticed melody of a quiet string quartet.

In fact, you'd hardly notice it at all. It does not interfere with or block your view of the river either upstream or downstream. (That would have been very much the case had Lutyens's proposed replacement for the Ha'penny Bridge ever been built, because the design was for a formidable, rather imperial structure quite out of scale with the river itself and with all the other bridges including O'Connell Bridge, the grandest of them.) Here is simple elegance itself, with steel and reinforced concrete working in pleasant harmony.

It was assembled offsite and lifted into place in no more than half an hour using the largest telescopic crane in the country.[1] It has been a success from the beginning. At a time of unprecedented economic boom, with the Celtic Tiger in full cry, it opened up both sides of the river. On the less fashionable north side, it gave access to and from the little Italian Quarter, a cluster of restaurants and other leisure facilities built by the developer Mick Wallace, who had been to the Italia '90 World Cup and decided on this initiative in homage to a culture with which he fell in love (although hardly the first person to be enchanted by *il bel paese*). The quarter survived the economic shock that followed the crash of 2008, although many similar places did not – the restaurant

Millennium Bridge with Lower Ormond Quay (*left*)

trade, in particular, is notoriously vulnerable to crisis – including some others in the adjacent area. The crash may have left the Italian Quarter intact, but it brought any further spread of benign development around here to a juddering halt, and that in an area that screamed out for renewal and the spread of some prosperity and good times across the river.

But it was precisely across the river, on the better established south side, that the Millennium Bridge earned its corn. It gave direct access to the centre of Temple Bar which, for all the many justified complaints about its specifics (far too many pubs, for example), was the first really successful exercise in urban social engineering in the history of the modern city, even pre-dating the heroics of the Custom House Docks Development Authority.

It had been recast with the principal aim of becoming Dublin's cultural quarter. We last met it in chapter 8, tracing its early development. But over the centuries its fortunes declined, and by the mid 1950s it was – along with much of the city – in poor shape, shabby, nondescript and unloved.

Prior to that, however, it had had its day. And its day, as with so much of central Dublin, was the eighteenth century. The opening of the old Custom House, on the site of what is now the Clarence Hotel, was the making of the area. As the principal clearing house for seaborne commerce – itself the very life blood and *raison d'être* of the city – a thriving, bustling commercial area developed around it. More dramatic parts of the expanding city were wonderful display places for the swank of the ascendant aristocracy, the places where the tourist buses still go today and where, oddly, you can find a strange urban tranquillity, as in the walk from the rear of Leinster House along Merrion Square South and down Upper Mount Street as far as the Grand Canal (which is delightful at this point but in truth not very grand, which may be why it is delightful).

Temple Bar was not at all like that. It was a centre of commerce, and artisanal commerce at that, with all the ancillary trades associated with shipping present and correct: chandlers, customs agents, caulkers and so on. And prostitutes. Temple Bar in the eighteenth century was one of the centres of the trade in Dublin, a city otherwise well provided for in this regard.

But the closure of the old Custom House and its removal downriver to be housed in Gandon's magnificent new building on the north bank of the river at what was then the eastern margin of the city began the decline of Temple Bar. That was in 1791. The great engine of the area's vitality was now gone, and with it went Temple Bar's commercial urgency. These things are seldom sudden; it was gradual decline, from urgent vitality to marginality.

But the twentieth century – or most of it – was a story of shameful neglect. By the 1970s, it was shabby, bypassed, a grim little grid of small, nondescript streets with no visible urban purpose. All this more or less plumb in the city centre: where's your pride, indeed. This was not helped by a pharaonic *grand projet* thought up by CIÉ, the publicly owned national transport company.

The idea was to create a road transport hub in Temple Bar, with the city's principal bus station to be located there. To this end, CIÉ bought up small properties in the area as they came on the market with a view to consolidating the lot into the terminus thus mooted. The effect, of course, was to hasten the decline of an already declining district. Nobody was going to bid for vacant or available properties if this behemoth was casting its shadow before it. Moreover, the company also proposed to buy up similar properties on the north side of the river with a view to joining the two by a railway tunnel under the Liffey which might, on some projections, be somehow extended to Tallaght in the far south-western suburbs.

Quite what was going to be used for money in all this was never entirely clear, this at a time when Ireland generally was on its uppers financially. Nor did too many people give any serious consideration to the effect of a vast expansion of road traffic in this sensitive locale. Although the principal plan was for a bus station, any such development – especially if the north-side bit were to be completed, was bound further to increase road traffic use. The city centre would have to be further remade for cars and lorries as well as buses, at God knows what cost to the urban fabric.

It never happened. Politics matters, and it was politics that saved the city from the bureaucratic juggernaut. Activists and small traders who had moved into the area on short-term leases – anything else made no sense – started to lobby the Dublin Corporation, as it still was then, to use grants and tax breaks to turn the area into a bohemian and creative quarter instead. The lobby reached the ear of the government, then under the direction of the sinister, corrupt but occasionally imaginative Charles Haughey. Charlie affected to be a grand patron of the arts and he certainly put more value on *kultur* than the general run of Irish politicians – although that is not saying a lot.

Haughey made CIÉ retreat and effectively abandon its *grand projet*. Instead, the government committed IR£15 million to an urban regeneration scheme designed to create a cultural quarter in Temple Bar. There were matching funds (and more) for urban regeneration coming on stream from Brussels at this time, to the tune of IR£22 million. The EU, as it was shortly to become, was anxious to encourage urban renewal projects of this kind, so that obviously helped and confirmed the government in the virtue of its new commitment.

This all led to the establishment of Temple Bar Properties, a not-for-profit public–private partnership in 1991. Its purpose was to facilitate this grand plan, which mixed residential developments – mainly apartments – with entertainment outlets – mainly pubs and restaurants – and cultural nodes such as small theatres, an artists' centre, the National Photographic Archive of the National Library plus a Gallery of Photography, and similar enterprises. A book market and a food market developed in time, as if spontaneously but actually under public licence. One hand washed the other, and Temple Bar did indeed become Dublin's cultural quarter, a magnet for tourists (not always the type of tourist desired by the high-minded) and in general the city's central play space.[2]

It is all too easy to deplore the excessive number of pubs and the consequent drunkenness that became too common a feature of the district. The people's idea of *kultur* did not always run to Beckett and Cartier-Bresson as much as to Arthur Guinness and John Jameson. This was a common disappointment for idealistic planners who do indeed incline to high-mindedness, as with the early days of radio, television and the internet, optimistically supposing that a rising cultural tide will lift all idealistic boats but paying insufficient attention to the actual preferences of the demos, who generally prefer instant gratification to more cerebral preoccupations.

But for all that – so well-rehearsed by now as to be tedious – the renewal of Temple Bar, more than any other benign development in the city since the 1980s, is a model of how any city might remake itself. It was helped by that old standby – location. Unlike Smithfield or the lower quays, it was ideally placed, in a part of the city for which there was real potential simply because people wanted to be there. They were all around; it was now just a matter of building on the presence of those people and offering something different. This was done: the area was recast with well-designed new buildings and open spaces and, in one case, an entirely new street. The whole compact area, bounded by Dame Street to the south, Westmoreland Street to the east and Winetavern Street to the west – with the new civic offices adjacent – and the river, quickly developed a personality, vivid, playful, rowdy and fun, that marked it off from the rest of Dublin while at the same time becoming an indispensable part of it. It's a pity about the drunken excesses but the contrast should surely be with the inert dead-end quarter it was before Haughey hit CIÉ's brakes.

All that was south of the river. It was a rather different story

Widely regarded as Dublin's cultural quarter, Temple Bar is a model of how any city might remake itself

on the other side. Temple Bar had one advantage over all: it was established and thriving before the great financial crash of 2008. So it took a beating but survived. The north side of the Millennium Bridge gives on to Lower Ormond Quay near Jervis Street. In the days before the crash, much of this area immediately behind the quays became a subdued clone of Temple Bar. But even at its best, it was never more than a thin membrane of new fashion running parallel to the river for barely half a block back to Great Strand Street, after which the energy quickly ran out. Abbey Street, one entire block back in, never really caught the new current. Indeed, the only place that echoed Temple Bar, an L-shaped complex called the Great Epicurean Food Hall with entrances on Lower Liffey Street and Middle Abbey Street, did not survive the financial storm.

So there are splendid things hereabouts – the Italian Quarter and some really good restaurants on the quays themselves – but the area has developed no collective personality similar to Temple Bar. Abbey Street remains what it has always been, mainly a rather dull commercial thoroughfare with few buildings of any distinction. The farther north you press, away from the river, the more pronounced this pattern becomes. This is mainly a shopping area of no great character. The one exception to all this is Capel Street, the principal north–south thoroughfare leading to its eponymous bridge. In recent years, it has had a conscious makeover and in the opinion of many is now the most interesting street in the city centre. Again, this has been driven by sensitive planning rather than by the demands of the market.

Still, the Millennium Bridge links two unequal parts of town. Temple Bar is *sui generis* and any attempt to extend its reach, in a kind of urban *mission civilisatrice*, simply meets conditions which didn't exist in Temple Bar. It was a sort of blank slate on which planners could extend themselves. The north side is a crowded commercial and retail area, and opportunities for big ideas are correspondingly limited. This makes the renewal of Capel Street all the more admirable because it is tactful and understated.

It is historically appropriate that this should have happened, for as we saw (chapter 4) this is the spine of the modern city. All the marvellous and swift development of the north side, from the 1670s through the eighteenth century, came from here. So the fact that its renewal has retained its essential character – a little flyblown and not at all grandiose – is to the credit of all concerned. It was all around here that the modern city started. So while fashion has long since moved south – since the building of Carlisle/O'Connell Bridge in the 1790s, decisively and irreversibly so – Capel Street retains its quirky, somewhat boho character while getting a kind of short back and sides, a modest tidy-up.

The Millennium Bridge is in many ways the most aesthetically pleasing and discreet of all the Liffey bridges. O'Connell Bridge is nonpareil, but the rest of them are for the most part unremarkable, with the exception of the next bridge we shall examine, which is remarkable for all the wrong reasons, and later (chapter 19) the Sam Beckett Bridge, which is remarkable for all the right reasons. The Liffey, as we have seen, is no great urban waterway. It is a narrow river, requiring only modest bridging. As we saw earlier in this chapter, the Millennium Bridge is barely 40 metres across; Westminster Bridge is 250 metres, the Thames in central London being more than six times the width of the Liffey. So this quiet, restrained structure is well fitted to its location and to its role. There is no need to shout.

Which brings us, unfortunately, to the James Joyce Bridge upriver, which is all shouting. Here is the most conspicuous public artefact dedicated to a writer of genius in the city that he memorialised like no other. And it is all wrong.

— ✺ —

SEVENTEEN

JAMES JOYCE BRIDGE

Y ES, IT'S DESIGNED by Calatrava – or at least the studio of Calatrava. I am a huge admirer of Santiago Calatrava, architect, engineer, designer. He has designed bridges of stunning beauty and practicality all over the world: in Seville, Buenos Aires, even Venice – where his new bridge across the Grand Canal is a masterpiece of tact in what is probably the most sensitive site in the world. And in Dublin, too. His Sam Beckett Bridge downriver (chapter 19) is perfectly wonderful, the most dramatic of all the Liffey river crossings. It's at a point on the estuarial billowing of the river that can accommodate drama, and Calatrava delivers this with gusto.

But here, upriver between Queen Street and Bloody Bridges, stands a rank failure lacking all tact and discretion. The river is narrow here and its bed exposed and sordid at low tide. The last thing that a bridge here requires is drama. Yet that is what we have got. The James Joyce Bridge is horribly out of proportion with everything around it – and out of sympathy, too. It looks as if it has been wilfully shoehorned into a neighbourhood where it is not wanted.

James Joyce Bridge – the less said, the better

What is it for, at all? Well, traffic flow again, principally. Like Queen Street Bridge adjacent, it carries traffic north to south to complement the Frank Sherwin Bridge downriver a bit which carries traffic south to north. Whether a bridge is needed here at all is still an open question, given that the bridges either side of it carry north to south traffic. And Queen Street Bridge at least leads somewhere once you are across it: not just the south quays heading for Heuston Station and the western suburbs but also south up along Bridgefoot Street to Thomas Street and the Liberties. The James Joyce Bridge just carries you to a T-junction on the south quays, yet another point of access for Heuston and the west.

This is Usher's Island, at the south quay abutments of the James Joyce Bridge. Of course, it is not an island, but the name recalls the actual island that stood in the river at this point before embankment, when its unruly natural course remained undisturbed. But that was a long time ago. Indeed, the very word 'island' is rather confusing because it conjures up an image of a body of dry land above the high-tide line sitting in the middle of the river. This is no help at all because, apart from anything else, there was not, as far as these things can be reconstructed by historical inference, an island in the middle of the stream.

So what was there? It appears that the island was indeed formed by a number of natural features but close to the south bank of the Liffey, so that its insular status was real but undramatic. It seems to have been formed by the natural flow of the Camac river, a small watercourse running in from Inchicore and Kilmainham and at this point flowing parallel to the Liffey. It ran east as far as a small pool called Usher's Pill, just west (upstream) of Fr Mathew/Church Street Bridge. To confuse matters, man-made watercourses were run off the Camac to serve as mill-races, all entering the main river at different points before the whole lot – Camac and all – were culverted and covered in as the south quays were developed in the eighteenth century. One of the man-made mill-races, the one that gave on to the Liffey near Bloody Bridge, marked the western end of the island. The eastern end, Usher's Pill, had been filled in much earlier, in 1685.

In effect, Usher's Island was the westward extension of the urban holdings of the Usher family at Bridgefoot Street – a long garden. But it all started from the Usher house on that street, so that its island status was – until the culverting – modest, being little more than a projection of terra firma westward with the Camac serving for a while as a southern boundary. The denomination of the place as an island, while literally correct until all the filling-in began, is the source of the nomenclatural confusion. So I hope that's all nice and clear now.

The key to the whole thing was the Usher property, firmly anchored in their south-shore house. They were a family of the utmost distinction, maintaining a long, continuous presence in Dublin. The earliest mention of the surname dates to 1302, when one John le Usher was appointed constable of Dublin Castle by King Edward I. One of his descendants, Arland Usher (or Ussher), was an established merchant in the town in the fifteenth century and one of his descendants, John Usher, had the distinction of financing the publication of the first book ever printed in the Irish language, in 1571.[1] In the twentieth century, another Arland Ussher – the orthography is variable – maintained his family's literary link not only by himself being a distinguished man of letters but also by rendering, in 1926, the first published translation of Brian Merriman's wonderful bawdy poem *Cúirt an Mheán Oíche/The Midnight Court*. Along the way, James Ussher (1571–1656), Anglican Archbishop of Armagh and Primate of All Ireland,[*] was one of the first to graduate from the College of the Holy and Undivided Trinity of Queen Elizabeth near Dublin, known to us simply as Trinity. On a cadet branch of the family, one of its descendants was Arthur Wellesley (1769–1852), Duke of Wellington and victor of Waterloo.

So by the early eighteenth century, the two south-side quays – Usher's Quay to the east just upriver of Church Street Bridge and Usher's Island Quay, its continuation to the west – were well-established as a pleasant riverine suburb. It was here, at number 15, that James Joyce's grand-aunts lived and here that he set his great short story 'The Dead', the last story in *Dubliners* and, in the opinion of many, the finest short story in the English language.

---

[*]   Some branches of the family conformed at the Reformation; others didn't, which left them on the back foot socially and materially.

The house was shamefully neglected for decades by the city authorities, then rescued when a private citizen bought it and did essential structural repairs. Then it was proposed to turn it into a hostel, a proposal that met with protests from literary people who wished, very reasonably, to have this exceptional location turned into a cultural centre for the benefit of all. It is hard to imagine any other city anywhere treating the memory of its greatest writer so casually.

Usher's Island Quay was, however, for a long time a dead end. It was not until the opening of Kingsbridge/Heuston Station a little further to the west in 1846 that there was any need to extend it further; the development of Victoria Quay achieved that purpose, although the long curtain wall serving as the boundary of the Guinness Brewery renders it a rather featureless stretch of thoroughfare.

One of the unintended consequences of the building of Victoria Quay was the removal of the Richmond Tower, a Gothick piece of faux medieval/faux Tudor street furniture, from its original site at the bottom of Watling Street. It was in the way. Quite what it was doing there in the first place is not altogether clear, other than as a form of decoration. But George Petrie's contemporary drawings show it as very decisively marking the end of the trail at the farthest western end of Usher's Island. In that terminal context, it makes some sense. But as Petrie's work makes abundantly clear, its position sitting right down on the riverbank made further development along the south quays impossible. With the coming of the railway – which just about upscuttled all existing arrangements everywhere – it suddenly became a nuisance. What is now Victoria Quay was still unembanked, and was to remain so until the quay was developed, so that the

Richmond Tower came right down to the abutment of Bloody Bridge, as Petrie shows.

So it was moved to its present location at the western entrance to the Royal Hospital grounds, opposite Kilmainham Gaol. The tower had originally been built at the bidding of the city authorities and designed by Francis Johnston in the then modish Gothick style, unlike most of Johnston's work, which was either classical or Graeco-Roman, as in the case of his most celebrated building, the General Post Office in O'Connell Street. It was named, with weary predictability, for the lord lieutenant, the duke of Richmond, who performed the official opening in 1812. But by 1846 it was in Kilmainham, and Victoria Quay was being punched through to Kingsbridge Station.

We have wandered a bit upriver from the James Joyce Bridge. If the bridge ends in a T-junction at Usher's Island on the south shore, it leads directly into Blackhall Place on the north. This in turn takes you into Stoneybatter and Manor Street, at the end of which the inner suburbs begin to announce themselves. But this small area has become one of the most compelling districts in modern Dublin, defying the prevailing idea that the north-west quadrant is doomed to be forever unfashionable. For Stoneybatter, Manor Street and modern Oxmantown are hip and home to the bobos.

This is all a pretty recent development, for the area was not always cool. In fact, for about two centuries it shared the fate of the north-west of the city generally and was thought undesirable. It had, in Gaelic days before the coming of the Vikings and Normans, been the principal thoroughfare out of the town on this side, heading off into the countryside in County Meath, including the royal site at Tara. There was a village here known as *Bóthar na gCloch* (the road of the stones, thus its later anglicisation as Stoneybatter). But in addition to the general misfortunes of the district, the building of the enormous Royal Barracks (now Collins Barracks) nearby in 1701 did nothing to improve it. To the contrary, as we saw earlier, the barracks attracted all sorts of low life – not least prostitutes – in its shadow. Stoneybatter became 'a receptacle for wickedness and a harbour for varlets'.[2]

The barracks stood at the western end of what had historically been Oxmantown Green, running roughly from Church Street all the way to the Phoenix Park. It was gradually eroded as bits of it were nibbled away by speculators like William Ellis (chapter 3), by the development of Smithfield as a market area and by the barracks itself. What made it in its modern form was the Dublin Artisans' Dwelling Company (DADC), founded for philanthropical purposes in 1877 but run as a disciplined business, expecting a return on funds committed. It was no charity and was tightly managed. As the name implied, it was designed to provide decent housing for skilled workers – the unskilled majority remained in their loathsome tenements until the great state-led slum-clearance programmes of the years after independence.

The DADC's biggest project was here, in the Stoneybatter/ Manor Street/Oxmantown district, the latter now referring exclusively to this reduced area. In this area of 28 acres, between Manor Street and Oxmantown Road, the company built over a thousand houses in the first decade of the twentieth century.[3] It was only later in the century, when these houses came on the private purchase market, that young professionals and such like – the bobos, being priced out of other areas by escalating property prices – settled it.

It was a classic case, perhaps the most obvious in modern Dublin history, of gentrification. The old artisanal working class for whom the area was first developed by the DADC yielded to the upwardly mobile, many of whom earned their crust in media, advertising and similar vocations. It even has its own publishing house, the Lilliput Press, a small but very distinguished enterprise. Stoneybatter is cool.

None of this, unfortunately, has much to do with the James Joyce Bridge, which just happens to be on its doorstep. Most of this book has attempted to trace the consequences of the various Liffey bridges going up, of the effect that each bridge has had on its immediate hinterland. In the case of the James Joyce Bridge, this effect has been nil: what happened in Stoneybatter would have happened anyway and there was no causal link to the bridge. In that, as in everything else, the bridge is a useless, sorry thing.

All right, I'll stop now.

– ✿ –

EIGHTEEN

SEÁN O'CASEY BRIDGE

Now this is a lot more like it. We are way downriver again, below the Matt Talbot Memorial Bridge. The Seán O'Casey is a pedestrian bridge linking the Financial Services Centre on the north bank to City Quay on the south. Its design was won by the Irish architect Cyril O'Neill in an open international competition under the direction of the Custom House Docks Development Authority (CHDDA). O'Connor Sutton Cronin were appointed the consulting engineers; their work brought them the acclamation of their peers and a number of awards.

It's a swing bridge: its two sections open horizontally, although the mechanism failed for a while, causing much cynical hilarity until it was reprogrammed. It's also a slightly bouncy bridge: you can feel the mild spring underfoot as you cross it, like a number of similar pedestrian bridges elsewhere such as London's Millennium Bridge leading from Bankside and Tate Modern across to St Paul's and the City.

The Liffey has begun to widen towards the sea by now. The

span of the O'Casey Bridge is almost 100 metres. Compare that
to the Millennium Bridge, barely more than a kilometre upriver,
at a mere 40 metres, as we saw in chapter 16. The wretched James
Joyce Bridge has about the same span, so the river really has taken
on an estuarial feel by the time we get down below Butt Bridge.

This pedestrian bridge opened in 2005 and was named, very
appropriately, for the city's finest playwright, whose great Dublin
trilogy* has become an imperishable part of the Irish theatrical
canon. O'Casey, a working-class lad who left school at fourteen
years of age, received what little formal education he had in St
Mary's and St Barnabas's national schools nearby. When he wrote
of the lives of the Dublin tenement poor, he knew whereof he
spoke.

Yet the contrast between the lost world of O'Casey and the
modern city quarters either side of the bridge named for him
could hardly be more stark. O'Casey's theatrical world – well
grounded in sociological reality – was one of material deprivation
and social failure. The world of the bridge, particularly on the
north shore where it delivers you to the Financial Services Centre,
is utterly different. It is a poster child of the roar-away Celtic
Tiger, a reminder of the narrow margin between the material
successes (and excesses) of finance capitalism and what seems to
be an almost pre-programmed hubristic overreach.

None the less, it is the IFSC that inevitably catches the eye.
Well within living memory, this area was a wasteland. The story
of the IFSC is well-known and has been told in greater detail
elsewhere; it requires no more than the barest summary here. Like
the renewal of Temple Bar, a contemporaneous development, it was

---

* *The Shadow of a Gunman* (1923), *Juno and the Paycock* (1924) and his masterpiece
The Plough and the Stars (1926).

another case of politics mattering. And once again, the politician was Charles J. Haughey. He had negotiated an agreement back in 1982 with Tony Gregory, a left-wing independent for this constituency, whose parliamentary support he wanted following a tight general election. A deal was done which included a special economic development zone for the now redundant inner-city docks. His government did not last long but the idea of a special zone, complete with public funds and generous tax breaks for businesses setting up there, stayed with Haughey.

He returned in 1987 with a rather more secure majority and formed a government. The docklands enterprise zone that emerged might not have been quite what Gregory had had in mind; its actual form was influenced more by Dermot Desmond, a successful financier and a supporter of Haughey at a time when he needed all the support he could muster. The IFSC was established on a site bounded by Memorial Road to the west and Guild Street to the east, and from the river back towards Sheriff Street on its northern boundary. The extent was approximately 11 hectares, eventually expanding downriver beyond Guild Street to 38 hectares. It has become one of the most successful special enterprise zones in the country, although during the dizzy years towards the crescendo of the Celtic Tiger excesses it acquired a well-justified reputation as the 'Wild East' of European finance capitalism. It is, in many respects, a smaller country cousin of the post-Big Bang City of London: Canary Wharf on-the-Liffey.

But its effects – in commercial architecture, residential development and general civic infrastructure such as hotels, schools and the National College of Ireland, a business-orientated third-level institution – have been transformative. Imaginative and distinguished new buildings all along the quays have replaced the dereliction that had previously marked the area. The presence of new residential apartment areas for professionals has been especially notable, bringing a degree of settled life to an area previously written off as a social sink reserved only for the very poorest. (And the contrast with Sheriff Street nearby, poor although not as poor as hitherto, remains stark, as is the very obvious class and cultural divide.) Many professional support businesses, such as legal practices and accountancy and management advice services, moved from the traditional commercial centres around Dame Street and environs to this new enterprise area. It has not been an unqualified triumph but, a bit like Temple Bar, it is worth looking at it now and recalling what all this new-fangled development has replaced.

As you cross the Seán O'Casey Bridge, walking south to north from City Quay, the building directly in front of you is now badged as CHQ, the Custom House Quarter. It has a history.

As we saw in the Water Break chapter, this district is marked out for the first time in Rocque's map (1756) as Amory's Ground. The map shows the quay from what is now Memorial Road to Commons Street and beyond as set out in lots, all neatly delineated and awaiting development. Only thirty years earlier, Brooking (1728) had shown this as opened ground, marked as '[wall] not built as yet', but clearly planned, and the area Rocque showed as Amory's Ground was marked as still subject to tidal inundation. So we can take it that these years, from the 1720s to the '50s, were the ones in which development quickened hereabouts, this being consistent with what we have already seen elsewhere.

By the time of the Ordnance Survey Six-Inch Map of 1837, the whole area is well filled in and what is now the CHQ building – facing us as we walk across Seán O'Casey Bridge – is central to this process. The building marked the eastern boundary of the early Custom House Dock. It was built as a storage warehouse, mainly for tobacco, and when it was opened in 1821 was the largest clear floor space in Dublin. So it remained until the twentieth century. It stood 475 feet long (about the length of two football pitches back to back) by 157 feet wide, with extensive cellar vaults underneath for the storage of wines and spirits; the whole place was top lit.[1] It is a fine example of early industrial architecture in a city which, because of its essentially commercial rather than industrial purpose during the nineteenth century, is not exactly overflowing with examples.

It was unsurprisingly known as the Tobacco Store and later as Stack A, as similar warehouses were erected next to it. But their usefulness was relatively short-lived, for as we have already noted, this early dockland was superseded by further developments

Custom House Quay, c. 1880

downriver. The building also became known as the Banquet Hall, because its great space was able to accommodate a banquet which was provided to honour the huge number of Irish troops returning from the Crimean War in 1856.

The Crimean War was one of history's sillier conflicts. It arose from the ambition of Russia to extend its territory across the Black Sea and to grab some further lands from the decaying Ottoman Empire. But to do so would threaten Constantinople and the vital marine choke points at the Bosporus and the Dardanelles. If the tsar could have all these, he would have fulfilled a sense of religious mission by restoring the great city as the chief centre of Christian Orthodoxy after centuries of Muslim rule, only now it would be under Russian rather than Greek suzerainty. More to the point, as the French and the British saw things, it would also have given Russia control of the eastern Mediterranean, thus threatening Anglo-French trade routes, with the British especially itchy about India. (This became of even greater concern for the British a few years later with the opening of the great canal at the isthmus of Suez, which dramatically shortened the passage to India.)

So the French and the British set aside centuries of mutual antagonism and went to war against Russia, eventually succeeding. The conflict was fought out in the Crimean peninsula and was a hideous mess from beginning to end. Its most famous single incident was the Charge of the Light Brigade at the Battle of Balaclava, memorialised in one of Tennyson's windier poems that established itself at or towards the head of a fine British tradition – remembering a military collapse or fiasco as a heroic moment. In this case it was the fiasco that requires emphasis: it was one of the most stupid bungles in military history. Even by the standards of this muddled conflict on the edge of Europe, it stood out. In

Sergeant Luke O'Connor Winning the Victoria Cross at the Battle of Alma by Louis William Desanges, 1854

the Crimea overall, about 7,000 Irish troops died: the first-ever Victoria Cross was won there by an Irishman, Sergeant Luke O'Connor from County Roscommon (he ended his days as a general and a knight of the realm). At Balaclava, 114 of the 673 men who charged down the valley on garbled orders were Irish (as was the man who delivered the orders and the man who took delivery of them). Of the 118 killed that day, 21 were Irish. Of the 127 wounded, 21 were Irish. Of the 45 taken prisoner, 7 were Irish. Irish enlistment in the British colours was a tradition invested with considerable pride; it was only later in the nineteenth century, as the nationalist cause matured, that army recruitment became more troublesome.*

---

* Even at that, as late as 1914, in an age when Irish nationalism was in full flow, over 200,000 Irish volunteered for service in World War I.

So in 1856, when the troops came back to Dublin from
the Crimea, a grand banquet was thrown for them in this huge
warehouse on the Liffey quays. As they marched down the
quays to dinner, they were cheered by an enthusiastic crowd. The
banquet itself comprised thirty-two tables running the length
of the building (remember those two football pitches). Not only
were the men fed but so also were ancillary military – chaplains
and such like – together with sponsors and the sort of pot-bellied
great and good who invariably get seated at affairs of this kind
in every age.

There were consumed: 250 hams; 230 legs of mutton; 500 meat
pies; 100 venison pasties; 100 rice puddings; 260 plum puddings;
200 each of turkeys and geese; 250 servings of beef; 2,000 loaves
of bread; and three tons of potatoes. Plus drink: one Dublin wine
merchant donated 8,500 quart bottles of porter overall and a pint
of port each for the soldiers.[2] The whole thing lasted from about
11 a.m. to 4.15 p.m.

One of the reasons that Stack A was made available for this
blowout was that its original warehousing function had been
compromised by downriver developments. It remained standing,
of course, but all around it the inner docks were losing their *raison
d'être* with every passing decade. For the next century and more, it
was used as a kind of overflow warehouse for all sorts of seaborne
merchandise. In 1987, it came under the aegis of the CHDDA.
It was brilliantly reimagined as a leisure and retail space, a model
of how to modernise an historic building without robbing it of its
architectural authenticity. Moreover, it became the home of EPIC.

EPIC is a museum but is not what you visualise when you
hear the word 'museum'. It is a celebration of the Irish diaspora,
recalling that, while much of it began in tragedy and dispossession,

it has none the less created an extraordinary body of human achievement. It uses interactive digital techniques to illustrate (quite literally and graphically) its points. It is a celebration of the human achievement of a people which, at the lowest point in its history, comprised no more than 4.2 million people on the island itself. Of course, that figure disguises a lot, for it reflects the massive out-surge of people from Ireland in the wake of the Great Famine of the mid-nineteenth-century. That, in its turn, had accelerated a process already well in train since the middle of the eighteenth century.

It is understandable, if mistaken, to put the emphasis on the post-Famine emigration. But that is for a reason. This emigration – overwhelmingly from those parts of the country which later became the Republic of Ireland – ruined an entire society. The structure and social economy of Ireland outside Ulster were transformed by the departure of its poorest and most vulnerable people. What was left behind was a new structure of social organisation, in which the landlords – for almost two centuries the owners and stewards of the land, and therefore the beneficiaries of its politics – were progressively weakened; their larger tenants grew in relative prosperity and eventually themselves became the owners of the land. Towns gradually – very gradually – developed.

The pre-Famine emigration, roughly for the hundred years up to 1850, was not so consequential. It did not transform the pre-existing society. It was driven by two factors. In Ulster, social and religious antagonism between Presbyterian tenants and Anglican landlords brought the departure of large numbers of the former, usually to America. There, they established themselves on the western frontier of the Atlantic colonies, always looking to push ever further across the Appalachian Mountains into the rich valleys of the Ohio and Mississippi rivers, although in law these lands were initially reserved for Native Americans. Those laws were soon set aside; the ferocious Ulster Scots – as they became known – pressed their irresistible ambitions, and pressed them ever westwards. They eventually produced their own president and champion, Andrew Jackson, in the 1820s and '30s, and more of his kind thereafter.

In Ireland outside Ulster, sheer economics was a greater driver of pre-Famine emigration. The industrial revolution took off in England from about 1780. It offered work to unskilled Irish immigrants who were prepared – like all new arrivals – to undercut existing wage rates. This naturally made them hated at the lower end of English society. But the Famine, when it first came in 1845, greatly accelerated this process. Ireland was suddenly quite incapable of feeding its population even the modest diet of potatoes and buttermilk that had sustained it for decades. Ireland starved. A million died. Another million fled, some to England, to compound existing social tensions there, and many to America. An ambitious and relatively prosperous few who could afford the passage went to Australia – although many of the Irish who finished up there did so by dint of the courts of justice and the policy of transportation. Ironically, while not untouched, Ulster suffered least because the early industrial revolution had established itself in the east of the province – mainly in the Lagan Valley around Belfast – and this absorbed some of the destitute population of the countryside. However, in moving from country to town, people brought with them some of their old rural rivalries and hatreds, with grim prospects for the future social harmony of the province.

The total scale of Irish emigration in the second half of the nineteenth century is breathtaking. In 1851, towards the end of the Famine, the population of Ireland was 6.5 million; by 1911, it was down to 4.39 million. That's a loss of about a third in a single lifetime, as if France, for example, were to lose *20 million* people in our time. And, as we saw above, it continued to fall after that before a recovery came gradually after World War II. If you allow for a million who died directly of hunger or of Famine-related diseases, that still leaves a net loss of about 3 million people in a hundred years. No wonder there is a museum to celebrate the achievements of this diaspora, as well as to mark its tragedy. The wonder was only that it took so long to establish.

However, it is there now directly at the northern end of the Seán O'Casey footbridge, in the old Stack A tobacco warehouse which has been repurposed for it and for the other retail and leisure activities it hosts. EPIC is the brainchild of Neville Isdell, an Irishman who rose very high in the business world – he was chairman and CEO of the Coca-Cola Corporation when he retired. Although he had achieved his personal success outside Ireland, he had never lost his emotional connection to the land of his birth, and he put his good fortune behind this new museum.

Neville Isdell bought Stack A in 2013. The project he thus inaugurated conducted a number of feasibility studies about what such a museum might contain and how it might present itself. There was no initial public money committed but good relations were established with the public authorities; EPIC has now made itself an integral part of the Irish tourist mix. It was elected Europe's leading tourist attraction in 2019, 2020 and 2021. It has also made a singular contribution to the renewal of the north quays of the Liffey.

The story on the south bank of the river is more mixed – and somewhat more ambiguous. We have been walking across the Seán O'Casey Bridge south to north, heading not only towards Stack A/EPIC but towards the heart of a rejuvenated Custom House Dock area. Here there is the buzz and bustle of urbanity, especially during working hours. (Things quieten down a bit in the evening, as the various employees of the financial houses and the law firms – the majority who don't live locally – go home to the suburbs.) But turn around and start walking south. This is quite a different visual sensation.

When the bridge was being planned and the entire docklands area redeveloped under the aegis of the CHDDA, the authority took considerable care to consult the existing population of the area, which was inevitably going to be affected by the coming changes. Under the enabling legislation, they were obliged to do this: it was a statutory requirement, rather than a simple act of spontaneous generosity. As remarked earlier, this was to avoid a top-down elite of enlightened planners telling the locals what was good for them, especially if it was something that the locals did not want. The locals were poor and declining in numbers, but they were still there. By 2008, there were 17,500 people resident in the docklands.[3]

Inevitably, there were suspicions. The locals were understandably sceptical but gradually mutual trust was established, especially when the CHDDA personnel were gradually able to convince them of their bona fides and sincerity. What the locals wanted was pretty much what they got – and what they got was similar to what other inner-city populations, such as those on Summerhill and Portland Row, got when their areas were affected by changes. They wanted red-brick, suburban-scale semi-detached houses. In this case, the most visible developments were on City Quay and Lombard Street East.*

The problem is that word 'suburban'. This is a city centre, after all. It is not a suburb. Buildings that are disproportionate in scale – whether too big or too modest – are discordant here. I would feel the same way if a forty-storey skyscraper were proposed for this site, as has been proposed for a couple of sites nearby. These houses are simply too modest and too out-of-town for a site as sensitive as this. Just compare the visual effect of crossing this bridge from south to north to crossing it in the opposite direction. South to north, you are looking at the renewed area of Custom House Docks, with Stack A/EPIC directly ahead of you. Even if you don't approve, you must allow that this is a recognisably *urban* vista; you are downtown. At City Quay and Lombard Street, you could almost be in Dundrum. The sense of urbanity is diminished. There is a conflict between the palpable desire of local residents for one kind of streetscape and the reasonable expectations of what a city-centre milieu should look like. Imagine taking that perfectly pleasant three-bedroom semi from Dundrum and plonking it down on 5th Avenue and 59th Street or on the Champs-Élysées. It's rather like that +9, if you get my point.

This raises the larger question of Dublin's urban lack of visual coherence. Buildings are put up by a market-driven process in which the principal potential rewards will accrue to the entrepreneurial developers. Their concerns do not embrace visual architectural coherence. But the context in which these developments are considered and approved betrays the absence of any plan for the appearance of the city centre. That in turn betrays the absence of

---

* Lest Joyceans get confused, this is not to be confused with Lombard Street West, where Leopold Bloom lived for years. It is a different street, in a quite different part of town.

an overarching political authority: Dublin is not a self-governing entity. It depends on the exertions of administrative officials, who have no power to raise finance and must subsist on what central government doles out to them, which is never enough. (I am not naïve in hoping that a directly elected urban authority, with fiscal powers, under the direction of a democratically elected mayor – as in Paris and New York – would suddenly produce an enlightened governing class; just as likely it would produce the sort of political hacks and ward-heelers who have been representative of all Irish political systems in the democratic era. But it *might*, just *might*, be better than what we have now, which is visibly dysfunctional.)

This is the dilemma that must sooner or later be addressed, else Dublin will slide further into the sort of visual mediocrity that is all too representative of parts of the city, and of the city centre at that. I have already remarked on the state of the north inner city, which if anything is deteriorating even further despite occasional sticking-plaster patches here and there. There are plenty of examples on the other side of the river too: Patrick Street between the two cathedrals is simply a conduit for cars; the whole area immediately to the west of St Stephen's Green in the general direction of St Patrick's Cathedral is a jumble of buildings plonked down one next to the other but bearing no visual relationship of each to the other.

One recent writer, reviewing a history of Tudor England, noted that in the latter part of his reign, Henry VIII lacked 'the personal or practical capabilities to turn his many aspirations into reality'.[4] As with kings, scribblers. If you commissioned me to build another bridge over the Liffey, I wouldn't know where to start. I am sure that this is the only thing that I have in common with the late Hal – that I lack the personal or practical capabilities to turn my aspirations into reality. I am neither an architect nor a planner, but I am a Dubliner with a pair of eyes in my head. For all its faults, I have a genuine affection for my home town and wish it only to show some ambition. Where's your pride, eh? Where's your fuckin' pride?

– ✿ –

NINETEEN

SAMUEL BECKETT BRIDGE

AS TO PRIDE, this is the sort of thing I mean. The Samuel Beckett Bridge, last but one on the lower Liffey, is aesthetically stunning. The design is by Santiago Calatrava, and Calatrava at his best at that. And it's what I mean by a city having ambition. It is all too easy to sneer at 'statement architecture' but when it works it matters: who in the wide world gave a second thought to Sydney or to Bilbao before the Opera House or the Guggenheim? Of course, it can go wrong – hubris is a constant foe of all ambitious plans – but it has gone very right here, on the link from Sir John Rogerson's Quay to Guild Street on the North Wall. This may not be quite on the level of Sydney or Bilbao, but it expresses a similar sense of not settling for any old thing, or even second best. We have had too much of that in Dublin and we must be grateful that we don't have it here.

It is a cable-stayed bridge, with the stays supported by an elegant steel arc. In its turn, the arc is cable stayed to the abutment of the bridge on the south bank. The entire effect – whether or not it was deliberate, in recognition of one of Ireland's traditional symbols – is that of a harp lying on its side. The estuarial character of the lower Liffey is particularly felt here: the span is 123 metres, which gave Calatrava the kind of spatial oxygen he lacked at the James Joyce Bridge way upriver.

It is an opening bridge, allowing marine traffic to proceed further upriver. But its principal purpose is as a traffic bridge, providing a relief crossing for cars in particular on this stretch of the river. Such a crossing had been mooted in earlier plans for Dublin's urban development but never carried into execution. It is perhaps ironic that it was finally built and opened, in 2009, just as the centrality of the private car in urban transportation planning was coming under serious scrutiny for the first time in two generations.

As a traffic bridge, it has to be admitted that it is of limited utility. It certainly doesn't attract the weight of traffic that the €60m cost might justify. That said, it was worth every cent for the aesthetic effect alone. But its primary practical purpose has been compromised by its siting. Access from the south side is along Macken Street to Sir John Rogerson's Quay, at which point the driver has to enter a little chicane to access the bridge itself. This invariably involves traffic jams, especially at peak hours. Then there is the question of where it takes you: Guild Street is a bit of a dead end – not in the sense that no one wants to go there, although it seems that not enough do, but rather in the sense that there is insufficient demand for the relief that the bridge affords.

It is partly due to a policy of traffic management. A one-way system on the north side carries you irresistibly along Sheriff Street to the Five Lamps, with no right turn allowed towards the suburbs until Summerhill and Summerhill Parade. That's all right if you are going in the general direction of the airport, but it cuts out immediate access to the north-eastern suburbs; these can best be accessed by avoiding Sheriff Street using an acute right-hand turn through East Wall, effective but awkward. Still, it is not exactly a great incentive: drivers are notoriously prickly about what they consider unnecessary detours. While anyone can see that some expedients of these sorts are essential to any kind of disciplined traffic management – short of pharaonic or Haussmann-like destruction of existing settled areas in search of mathematically straight lines – these vexations are a disincentive to using the bridge.

It's less of a problem going from north to south, but still a bit clunky. Access to the bridge from Sheriff Street can be slow, and almost the entire weight of pontine traffic will then aim for Macken Street – there is very little to draw traffic further down along Sir John Rogerson's Quay, which means having to deal with the little chicane again.

All this can sound like grousing, especially given that I admire the bridge so much as a stunning piece of street furniture. I wish it were not so, but the fact is that this magnificent structure does not properly fulfil its primary, intended practical function.

What it does do is further enhance the revival of this part of the lower river. For all its bravura, it fits in well. On the North Wall side, it meets the National Convention Centre head on: a great tilted drum, this, at a reclining angle of about 30 degrees to the vertical just at the point where the Royal Canal enters the Liffey, having concluded its long, leisurely progress through the midlands from the Shannon. The Convention Centre is the nearest thing to a statement building on either side of the river, flanked as it is by new buildings – mainly offices of one kind or another for finance houses and professional practices parasitic

Samuel Beckett Bridge is Santiago Calatrava at his very best

upon them – that are themselves pleasing for the most part but not shouty. They have been accused of mediocrity, which only goes to prove Brendan Behan's observation that 'there's no playsin' some bastards', but to my eye they manifest that sense of visual coherence so lacking elsewhere in the city. The revival of the Liffey docklands has been a success – not an unqualified one, but the balance sheet is overwhelmingly positive.

If you cross the bridge going south and wiggle through the chicane to access Macken Street, you drive past the back of the Grand Canal Theatre.* You'd hardly notice it – it is, after all, the back of the building. Nor would you be aware that its front gives onto the revived Grand Canal Dock just a few metres away, one of the absolutely triumphant pieces of urban renewal superintended by the CHDDA. It is a really outstanding public space and the theatre is its linchpin. The architect – starchitect – is Daniel

---

* The naming rights have been sold to An Bord Gáis, the energy provider. I don't approve of naming rights – what next: the Durex Arc de Triomphe? – and therefore propose to stick with the original name of this splendidly civic building.

Libeskind, whose work on the whole leaves me cold, for all his international celebrity. But this theatre is a technical and aesthetic triumph, accommodating itself to a fiendishly cramped space with considerable elegance.

The plaza at Grand Canal Harbour has, sadly, nothing to do with the Sam Beckett Bridge, which just happens to be nearby. One did not prompt or cause the other, so no claim can be made for the bridge in that regard, such as can be made for Capel Street or O'Connell Bridges, to take the most obvious examples, without which the surrounding areas would not be as they are.

This bridge has made nothing happen, yet it fits in perfectly in context as though it had been a part of some grand plan. Given this, and its limited usefulness as a traffic relief route, it may be regarded as a folly. Well, three cheers for follies.

– ❀ –

TWENTY

ROSIE HACKETT BRIDGE

T HE MOST RECENT bridge on the river is a crossing for public transport only. Its principal function is to carry the Luas green line southbound. It also has two lanes for buses and taxis. So it is a virtuous little bridge.

The Luas is an excellent two-line tramway (the lines intersect at Lower Abbey Street, just north of the bridge). It is well patronised, justifying its existence by public use despite the quondam grumblings of bean-counters bothered by the capital cost of installing the infrastructure. The two lines, green and red, run roughly north–south and east–west. The green line divides between Trinity and Parnell Square, with the northbound track running along O'Connell Street and the southbound one block to the east along Marlborough Street. It is from this street that it needs to cross the river, and to get it across the Rosie Hackett Bridge was built.

The last stop before the bridge is simply called Marlborough but it is as good a place as any to start to talk about Dublin and trams. This part of the street is nondescript. No building stands out, other than one that may casually catch the eye across the street as you are waiting for the Luas to arrive. The reason it may do so is that, unlike all its neighbours, it is red-brick, although otherwise unremarkable. This was the headquarters of the Dublin United Tramway Company (DUTC), the first urban transport network in the city's history.

The idea of moving large numbers of people from A to B is a very modern one, being one of those things of recent historical development that we take utterly for granted as if having been there since time immemorial. To the contrary, it is an offshoot of the railway – yes, the railway again, that unfailing engine of modernity. Prior to the coming of the iron road, there was no way to move people in numbers on land. (Shipping was a different matter.) The best option was the stagecoach, necessarily limited in capacity to single figures or so, and only then for those who could afford them. The best-known example of a coaching operation in Ireland was that of the Italian entrepreneur Carlo Bianconi (1786–1875), whose network in the south and west was enormously successful and was sold on by him to his employees as a going concern as late as 1865, despite the inroads being made by the railway.

But the railway showed that you could move people in their hundreds. Tramway systems were a lateral extension of this realisation. The railway itself coincided with – and helped to develop – the enormous expansion of cities in the nineteenth century. Even sclerotic Dublin was not immune to this phenomenon, growing its population from about 200,000 in 1800 to 400,000 a century later. As cities grew bigger and, in cases like London and Dublin, followed the spatial sprawl so typical of British cities, the urban distances increased and the need for urban mobility became an issue. The railway itself could satisfy some of this need but only in part; it was possible, as on the route of the Dublin and South Eastern to Bray, to stud commuter stops along the way for any person who, having escaped to the suburbs, now needed to get back in and out of town for work.

That was fine where there was a pre-existing railway. Where there wasn't, the capital cost of providing one from scratch was prohibitive; tramways were cheaper to develop and – as the DUTC was to demonstrate – capable of generating good operating profits and paying a handsome dividend to shareholders. The alternative was the omnibus but it could not match a tram for numbers. That said, two of the great cities of the century, London and Paris, opted for buses rather than trams while developing underground railways earlier than most. But New York developed its streetcar system early, using existing stagecoach routes: the first one dated from as early as 1832, when the New York and Harlem opened its horse-drawn route along 4th Avenue.* In Dublin, the first form of urban public transport came in the second half of the 1830s – significantly, just in the wake of the railways, emphasising yet again what a shift of mindset the railway induced – when a horse omnibus service appeared. A horse-drawn bus system developed in the subsequent decades, echoing London, but it soon became clear that buses were an incomplete answer. What was needed was a fixed-rail system; the first tram tracks were laid in the early 1870s and the first horse-drawn trams ran from College Green

---

* K.T. Jackson, ed., *The Encyclopedia of New York City*, Yale UP, 1995. The streetcars gave a new word to the language. In the second half of the nineteenth century, baseball became the consuming urban recreation in America; its fans hurried to the ball park, dodging between the streetcars, thus earning them the name of 'tram dodgers', which became the official name of the Brooklyn Dodgers (now the Los Angeles Dodgers, the franchise having been moved west in the 1950s).

The predecessor to Luas, the DUTC had 280 trams working 60 miles of active line
at its peak

via St Stephen's Green and Rathmines to Terenure on 1 February
1872.[1]

During the rest of that decade, a cat's cradle of tramway
development companies laid track all over the city: a line east–
west from Kingsbridge (Heuston) Station to Earlsfort Terrace and
then lines south to Sandymount and Donnybrook, Rathmines,
Clonskeagh, Inchicore, Blackrock and Kingstown. To the north,
track was laid to Glasnevin, Drumcondra and Clontarf. These were
generally developed by separate companies, but in 1881 many of
them were consolidated into a single company, and by 1896 that
process had been completed with the formation of the DUTC.

Its leading figure was William Martin Murphy, a buccaneering
capitalist originally from West Cork, where he was part of a
politico-business network remembered ever after as the 'Bantry
Gang'. He had married the daughter of one James Fitzgerald

Lombard,* a property developer originally from County Kerry who, along with his partner John McMahon, had developed residential properties on both sides of the river: on the south side around Heytesbury Street and on the north in Drumcondra and environs. Indeed, he was instrumental in securing independent township status for Drumcondra, the last of the townships to be so designated, in 1879.

It is interesting the number of energetic provincials who drove Dublin commercial life in this period. Apart from Lombard and Murphy, there was also Patrick Joseph Plunkett from County Meath who developed many of the red-brick south-side suburbs and made a fortune that allowed his son George to live a life of scholarly, gentlemanly ease: he is better remembered as George Noble, Count Plunkett, father of Joseph Mary Plunkett, one of the leaders of the Easter Rising of 1916 executed in its aftermath. The title, a hereditary one, was awarded to George by the pope in 1884 for contributions to Catholic charities.

But such men were few in a city generally depressed economically, which is part of the reason why William Martin Murphy shone such a vivid light. He was the sort of free-wheeling, ruthless capitalist to be found in abundance in contemporary Manhattan but whose rough energies disturbed somnolent Dublin. There is no doubt that he was a businessman of the first ability, and perhaps Dublin was too small a stage for him: certainly it was not just his enemies in the labour movement – James Larkin above all – who hated what they considered his bumptiousness, his insensitivity and his authoritarianism. Many of his fellow-businessmen, genteel by comparison, found him hard going. But

---

* Lombard stood at the head of a long tradition of Dublin property developers from west of the Shannon, often reviled as philistine money-grubbers insensitive to urban life.

it was difficult to argue with his undoubted intelligence and drive.

He was forever notorious for his part in the great Dublin lockout of 1913, when he gave his DUTC employees a stark choice between abandoning their membership of Larkin's union or their jobs. Heroically, they stayed solid for the best part of six months, refusing to submit to Murphy's bullying, before effectively being starved back to work in the early weeks of 1914. Murphy's name and memory have been mud in Dublin memory ever since, while Jim Larkin has a statue in O'Connell Street.

But there is no denying that Murphy's tramway network was one of the most impressive urban transport successes in Europe. He had been to the United States where he saw the effectiveness of electric traction, brought it to Dublin and dispensed with horses. By 1914, the DUTC was carrying fifty-eight million passengers per annum and the network covered most of the city centre and the developed inner suburbs.[2]

Murphy died in 1919, and after his death the DUTC began its decline. It was not so much the absence of his guiding hand as something that no businessman could have prevailed against: a huge technological change that introduced the internal combustion engine and spelt doom for all fixed-rail systems of transport. The long decline of the railways began at this time and for the same reason. By the 1920s, the signs were already there, and in 1949 the last DUTC tram ran. Track was torn up and the triumph of the bus, the lorry and the car was complete for the moment.[*]

But by the early 1990s, it was clear that this triumph was bought at an unsustainable price. Apart from developing

---

[*] One sentimental exception was the Hill of Howth tram, which went all the way up to the summit of the Hill of Howth. It lasted until 1959 but was not part of the DUTC network, the service being a subsidiary of the Great Northern Railway Company.

environmental concerns about exhaust emissions on air quality in the city, there was the simple brute fact that there was only so much road to accommodate what was a never-ending expansion of private cars in particular. Where were they to go? You could, of course, build more roads through the city, but public sentiment was ever more resistant to seeing historic neighbourhoods gouged through to create what were in many cases very temporary relief routes for drivers. Furthermore, the more roads you built – a slow, slow process in itself, what with all the legal and planning issues involved before anyone put a spade in the ground – the faster car sales accelerated to fill the space created, leaving the original problem back where it had been.

Moreover, public transport in numbers was back on the public screen. The success of the DART (Dublin Area Rapid Transit, 1984), which entailed electrifying the existing coastal railway lines as far north as Howth and Malahide and south as far as Bray (and later Greystones) with modernised rolling-stock was an eye opener. Just one commuter rail line, thirty-one stations, but twenty million passengers!

Suddenly, as it seemed, fixed track systems were back in fashion, or at least in the realm of the possible. For years, all such talk had been confined to the wilder shores of the green left, to whom policy-makers paid no attention. But a report dating from 1981 had recommended that a tramway system be revived as part of the urban mix. It was not a great decade for such recommendations of public provision: as we saw (chapter 15), there was no political will to curb people's right, as they saw it, to drive where they wanted. It took time to shift that mindset but the Luas tram system – just the two lines, crossing in the city centre – did get built and opened in the early years of the twenty-first century.

Since opening in 1984, the DART network has transported over 500 million passengers

But the north–south line needed to get across the river. Because the line divided at Trinity going north, the northbound track could, and does, use O'Connell Bridge. But the southbound track, coming along Marlborough Street, past the old headquarters of the DUTC, was stuck. Where Marlborough Street met Eden Quay on the north bank of the Liffey, there was nothing except the view across to Hawkins Street on the other side. That's why the bridge was built.

It opened in 2014 and was named for a worthy but almost totally forgotten labour activist and feminist. Rosie Hackett (1893–1976) is not a name that will be readily found even in sympathetic history books. The subcommittee of the City Council that recommended the naming had, at the time, a Labour majority and it was their act of piety that rescued the name from obscurity.*

---

* There is no biography of Rosie Hackett. Such biographical information as there is, for the most part, is contained in a series of specialist scholarly articles in academic journals. The best summary of her life is in the invaluable *Dictionary of Irish Biography*, one of the great works of collaborative scholarship in recent Irish history.

The choice divided opinion, not so much because she was a woman – even grizzled misogynists could hardly complain on that score – but because so few had ever heard of her. That made the choice either enlightened or wilful, according to taste. There were many who would have preferred the bridge to have been named for Lady Gregory, a much better-known woman whose Abbey Theatre is right beside it and whose contribution to Dublin and to Ireland none can gainsay.

It is yet another discreet, pleasant example of good bridge design. It does its job and does it without fuss or ostentation.

— ❧ —

ENVOI

WE ARE FINISHED with bridges. There has been a beginning, middle and end to these Dublin river crossings. Yet a book like this cannot pretend to be any kind of comprehensive history of the city. It does not touch the suburbs, except for the odd time when it can't help it. Instead, it traces the central seam, the binding that holds the whole town together and always has. Without the river, no city; without the bridges, God knows what.

Let us finish by widening the angle of vision which, in the nature of a work such as this, has of necessity been narrowly focused. Dublin wraps around its bay, making a huge letter C as it hugs the coast from Howth around past the mouth of the river to Dalkey and Killiney in the south. The Liffey bisects this curvature with a horizontal stroke, and its extension is the Great South Wall, projecting into the bay – beyond the reach of the river itself – giving the whole thing the effect of a euro sign (€). It is at the end of the wall, at the brick-red Poolbeg Lighthouse, that you get some wider perspective on all that we have considered thus far.

Standing here, you are no longer on the Liffey but on the margin of the Irish Sea into which the river has just folded behind you. Farther behind, upriver, is the city. Nearer, but still behind, is the port from which the outbound ferry that has just passed you has come. You can watch its receding stern as, like the city itself, it faces east. Just as you are facing east with the city and the ferry, just as Dublin has been doing since the first Viking longboat came hammering up this way more than a thousand years ago, you are gazing towards England.

Well, Wales actually.

NOTES

Introduction
1. de Courcy, *The Liffey in Dublin*, 343–4

1. Fr Mathew Bridge
1. Dickson, *Dublin: The Making of a Capital City*, 318

2. Islandbridge
1. *https://www.cso.ie/en/media/csoie/ releasespublications/documents/ statisticalyearbook/2004/ ireland&theeu.pdf*

3. Rory O'More Bridge
1. Craig, *Dublin 1660–1860: The Shaping of a City* (1952, 1969)
2. Bennett, *The Encyclopaedia of Dublin* (2005)

4. Grattan Bridge
1. Bennett, 59
2. Craig, 60

5. O'Donovan Rossa Bridge
1. Brady & Simms (eds), *Dublin: Through Space and Time*, 194
2. Boyd, *Dublin 1745–1922: Hospitals, Spectacle & Vice*, 126-9
3. Killeen, *Historical Atlas of Dublin*, 92
4. Craig, 47

6. Mellowes Bridge
1. Craig, 288
2. Craig, 179
3. Dickson, 83
4. Dickson, 214
5. *Irish Times*, 10 April 1997
6. *Irish Times*, 9 April 2011

7. O'Connell Bridge
1. de Courcy, 200
2. de Courcy, 275
3. McCullough, *Dublin: An Urban History*, 114
4. Brady & Simms, 149

8. The Ha'penny Bridge
1. de Courcy, 228–9
2. de Courcy, 114–15, 392–3

9. Heuston Bridge
1. Craig, 97
2. Brady & Simms, 174–5
3. de Courcy, 353
4. Ferris, *Irish Railways: A New History*, 20–2
5. Bennett, *The Encyclopaedia of Dublin*, 115
6. Craig, 300

10. Liffey Viaduct

1. Wolmar, *Blood, Iron and Gold: How the Railways Transformed the World* (2009)
2. Ferris, 140–1; de Courcy, 233, 308
3. Lennon, *Clontarf*, fig. 6, 18
4. de Courcy, 349
5. Lennon, ed., 9–10
6. de Courcy, 86, 349–50; Bennett, 200

11. Butt Bridge

1. de Courcy, 58
2. Gilligan, *A History of the Port of Dublin*, 11–14
3. Gilligan, 98
4. Pearson, 29–30; *Dictionary of Irish Biography*, entry on John Foster
5. de Courcy, 391
6. 6 McDonald, *The Destruction of Dublin*, 33

12. Loopline Bridge

1. *Dictionary of Irish Biography*
2. de Courcy, 236
3. Ferris, 53

13. Water Break

1. Gilligan, 89–90
2. *Dictionary of Irish Biography*; Gilligan, 148
3. Bunbury, *Dublin Docklands: An Urban Voyage*, 170
4. Craig, 91
5. Bunbury, 40

14. Frank Sherwin Bridge

1. *Dictionary of Irish Biography*

15. East Link

1. McDonald, 307
2. de Courcy, 137
3. Bunbury, 16ff
4. de Courcy, 377, who provides a very detailed account of the engineering history of the construction

16. Millennium Bridge

1. Pearson, *The Heart of Dublin: Resurgence of a Historic City*, 21–2
2. Dickson, 547

17. James Joyce Bridge

1. de Courcy, 401ff
2. Dickson, 123
3. Dickson, 396

18. Seán O'Casey Bridge

1. Bunbury, 48
2. Bunbury, 50–2
3. Bunbury, 17
4. Helen Hackett, *Times Literary Supplement*, no. 6238, 20

20. Rosie Hackett Bridge

1. Bennett, 64
2. Dickson, 387

6.

Dictionary of Irish Biography; de Courcy, 385; Gilligan, 115, 128, 140ff
7. *Dictionary of Irish Biography*; Dickson, 342–4

BIBLIOGRAPHY

Bennett, Douglas, *The Encyclopaedia of Dublin*, Gill & Macmillan, 2005

Boyd, Gary, *Dublin 1745–1922: Hospitals, Spectacle & Vice*, Four Courts Press, 2005

Brady, Joe and Anngret Simms (eds), *Dublin: Through Space and Time*, Four Courts Press, 2002

Bunbury, Turtle, *Dublin Docklands: An Urban Voyage*, Montague Publications Group, 2009

Craig, Maurice, *Dublin 1660–1680: The Shaping of a City*, Figgis, 1969

de Courcy, J.W., *The Liffey in Dublin*, Gill & Macmillan, 1996

Dickson, David, *Dublin: The Making of a Capital City*, Profile Books, 2015

Ferris, Tom, *Irish Railways: A New History*, Gill & Macmillan, 2008

Gilligan, H.A., *A History of the Port of Dublin*, Gill & Macmillan, 1988

Killeen, Richard, *Historical Atlas of Dublin*, Gill & Macmillan, 2011

Lennon, Colm, *Clontarf*, Royal Irish Academy, 2018

McCullough, Niall, *Dublin: An Urban History*, Anne Street Press, 1989

McDonald, Frank, *The Destruction of Dublin*, Gill & Macmillan, 1985

McGuire, James and James Quinn (eds), *Dictionary of Irish Biography*, Cambridge University Press, 2009

Pearson, Peter, *The Heart of Dublin: Resurgence of a Historic City*, O'Brien Press, 2000

Wolmar, Christian, *Blood, Iron and Gold: How the Railways Transformed the World*, Atlantic Books, 2009

ILLUSTRATIONS

Malton's View from Capel Street, looking over Essex Bridge, c. 1790 (*National Library of Ireland*)

Malton's A View of the Parliament House, College Green, c. 1790 (*National Library of Ireland*)

Grattan Bridge (*littleny/iStock*)

Malton's Tholsel, c. 1790 (*National Library of Ireland*)

O'Donovan Rossa Bridge (*Leonid Andronov/iStock*)

Liam Mellowes Bridge (*Leonid Andronov/iStock*)

O'Connell Bridge (*Bart_Kowski/ iStock*)

The Dublin Streets: A Vendor of Books by Walter Osborne, 1889 (*National Gallery of Ireland*)

O'Connell Bridge, c. 1960 (*Paul Popper/Popperfoto/Getty Images*)

Second colour section

George IV, King of England, entering Dublin, 1821, by William Turner (*National Gallery of Ireland*)

Seán Heuston Bridge (*powerofforever/ iStock*)

A view of the Dublin & Kingstown Railway from Blackrock, 1834 (*Science & Society Picture Library/ Getty Images*)

Ha'penny Bridge (*Bart_Kowski/iStock*)

Liffey Viaduct (*noel bennett/iStock*)

Butt Bridge and Loopline Bridge (*Derick Hudson/iStock*)

Matt Talbot statue by the Talbot Memorial Bridge (*Anne-Marie Palmer/Alamy Stock Photo*)

Dublin Port at night as seen from the East Link Bridge (*BartKowski/ Alamy Stock Photo*)

Millennium Bridge by night (*levers2007/iStock*)

James Joyce Bridge (*pictureproject/ Alamy Stock Photo*)

Seán O'Casey Bridge (*SAKhanPhotography/iStock*)

Opening of Rosie Hackett Bridge, 2014 (© *Dublin City Council*)

Samuel Beckett Bridge floats in Rotterdam (*GUIDO BENSCHOP/ AFP/Getty Images*)

Samuel Beckett Bridge and the Convention Centre (*sasar/iStock*)

Aerial view of River Liffey and city centre (*Guven Ozdemir/iStock*)

INDEX

A NOTE ABOUT THE AUTHOR

Fergal Tobin was a freelance writer and historian. His career was in publishing and he was president of the Federation of European Publishers in Brussels from 2010 to 2012. Under the pen name Richard Killeen he wrote several acclaimed works of Irish history, including *Ireland in Brick and Stone: The Island's History and Its Buildings*, *Historical Atlas of Dublin* and *The Concise History of Modern Ireland*. His previous book, *The Irish Difference*, was chosen as a Book of the Year by the *Irish Times*. Fergal died in February 2023, just after he finished writing *A City Runs Through Them*.